THE YOUNG PROFESSIONAL'S
SURVIVAL GUIDE

THE YOUNG PROFESSIONAL'S
SURVIVAL GUIDE

From Cab Fares to Moral Snares

C. K. Gunsalus

HARVARD UNIVERSITY PRESS
Cambridge, Massachusetts
London, England
2012

Library of Congress Cataloging-in-Publication Data

Gunsalus, C. K.
The young professional's survival guide : from cab fares to
moral snares / C.K. Gunsalus.
p. cm.
Includes bibliographical references and index.
ISBN 978-0-674-04944-4 (alk. paper)
1. Professional ethics. 2. Professional employees. I. Title.
BJ1725.G86 2012
174—dc23   2012020812

The Alma Mater statue on our campus says "To thy happy children of the future, those of the past send greetings." In that spirit, may the lessons of this book, gleaned from students of the past and my own children Kearney and Anna Shea, bring guidance to the young professionals of our future.

Contents

Survive What?

Imagine yourself in your new job. You've used your credit card to buy a new wardrobe and moved to a brand-new apartment, pushing the limits of your budget because it's so perfect for you. Then your boss asks—or worse, tells—you to do something that violates your sense of right and wrong. Or you find yourself making a choice at work that makes sense at the time, but that somehow you wouldn't want your family or friends to know about.

For society and our communities to function effectively, we depend on the idea that people should play by the rules, from stopping at stop signs to reporting financial information honestly. Over the years, all sorts of codes of conduct, written and unwritten, have gradually formed on top of the law and other rules governing society. These rules can be professional (what's an asset and what's a liability); scientific (notebooks must record research in real time and with absolute accuracy); social (table manners, the rules of soccer); honor based (it's not okay to pad your expense account even if "everybody else" is doing it); or practical (refill with gas before your car is running on fumes).

Which rules of the game really matter and which ones are mainly given lip service? How do you tell them apart? What if you see no good choices in a situation? How do you stay true to your own moral compass?

What do you do if your best friend, living in another state, in the midst of confiding a problem at work, tells you a confidential detail that will completely change a proposal your team has been working on for six months—and will reveal her as your source if you use it?

What if the members of your project team find key information that will help win a negotiation by peeking in your competitor's papers while he's taking a bathroom break? Would you be a fool to use the information, or a fool not to?

How do you decide if something you've been asked to do is wrong? What if you just don't know enough and it is not your place to ask questions? If your research supervisor instructs you to leave out data points that "muddy" the findings in a way you think is deceptive, even after you point out that leaving them out changes the reality of the results, what's your next step? Or if your supervisor tells you to write down any reason human resources will find acceptable, but never to hire any person over forty? How do you decide when to avert your gaze or quietly extricate yourself and when must you report the problem to the proper authority? How serious should it be before you raise questions or refuse to participate?

What if the response to your objections is, "Everybody does it"? What if everybody else *is* doing it?

How do you tell when you've crossed an ethical line and are just rationalizing? And what if you have only thirty seconds to decide?

Some choices are clearer than others. Sometimes there will be wrong answers though they may not always be obvious at the outset, other times you'll find yourself facing shades of gray, and there will be still others where there will be no single right answer and you'll have to assign priorities among completing right answers, as when you must choose between an important work commitment and an equally important family obligation, or between loyalty to a friend and your professional imperatives.

Almost no one sets out to do something embarrassing, wrong, or illegal. How do otherwise good people end up in trouble?

External forces and internal choices, alone or in combination, can lead there. Those around us affect us powerfully, so choosing where to work and with whom to affiliate is critical. And you will make choices.

In a study of the ethical dispositions of young workers, Howard Gardner—a MacArthur fellow and educator—directed a GoodWork Project at Harvard focused on ethical challenges faced by professionals to combine skillful and honorable work. He and his colleagues found that many of the young professionals they studied had "a well-defined sense of 'right' and 'wrong' but felt they had the right, while they were still young, to cut corners to advance their careers."[1]

But if you start taking shortcuts to get ahead, when will you stop? Is there ever a magical moment when you will wake up and decide, "Now I have enough [power, money, status, whatever] to be ethical"? Bending the rules puts us on a slippery slope: we coast until something goes wrong and then we collide with reality. We may suddenly find ourselves in unfamiliar territory, facing crushing and possibly game-changing consequences. How can you avert that kind of trajectory from the outset, and end where you want to be?

How you start will determine whether and how you will become the kind of professional you decide you wish. If you come to know yourself early on and develop a professional persona consistent with what you care about, you will have a dependable foundation for making the right choices going forward. You can learn, even in the absence of experience, to read warning signals, to use tools to help you avoid problems that can be avoided and handle those you do not, to put and keep yourself on the high road throughout your career.

Many of the problems that catch young professionals off guard are predictable. There will always be pressures, and there will always be incentives—to succeed, get promoted, get the bonus, get the right data, meet the quarter's goals, publish the right paper, win the sales competition. . . . Everyone has bosses above them and a next level to aspire to. Just remember that your colleagues will be taking cues from you just as you do from them. If you establish yourself as a person who does not cut corners and has high standards, you will likely be respected for it. It wasn't until the day I overheard someone say about me, "Don't ask her—you know she won't do it," that I saw how my behavior defined me. That was just fine with me. Aim to be one of those people who is not asked to cut corners in the first place.

Among the things I teach are a required course for all entering undergraduates at the University of Illinois College of Business called Business 101: An Introduction to Professional Responsibility, and the foundation ethics course for all MBA students, Leadership and Ethics. Throughout both of these courses, starting with the first day, I present students with a series of two-minute challenges, or 2MCs. A 2MC cannot necessarily be resolved in two minutes, though it usually requires a response in two minutes or less. The only way you can do that in the real world is to have thought about the issue, or one like it, ahead of time. The dilemmas in this book grow out of the 2MC approach to understanding and preventing problems at work: Each 2MC is based on a real problem encountered by a real person and most are based on the list of common pitfalls you can read about in Chapter 3. Using a standard decision-making framework, one we'll also explore here, in class we work through each 2MC, individually and in groups. Think of these 2MCs as dress rehearsals for situations that can and do arise in the working world.

I have spent my career dealing with the many ways people get themselves into trouble and building systems to prevent problems. I see people at the beginning of their careers in my classroom, and I see them at crisis points when something has gone terribly wrong and I'm investigating them or am part of an intervention that may signal the end of a career. The beginnings are a lot more fun and uplifting. The ends are what inspired me to write this book. Its lessons are rooted in practical skills and usable approaches to questions of ethics and professional responsibility. We'll explore them through the lens of real problems that happened to real people. The names and some details have been changed to preserve the central point without identifying their contributors.

Even if you follow every piece of advice in this book, you will not be able to keep hard problems from arising, but you can avert the avoidable ones and face the unavoidable ones on your own terms. How you make choices will affect how they play out. You're going to make mistakes. Everyone does. The key is to make mistakes from which you can recover. You can make that choice.

CHAPTER 1

Start As You Mean to Go On

You are all ready to go to work. You have filled out all the paperwork, found a place to live, figured out your transportation, gotten a haircut, and bought an extra alarm clock. You feel good to go. But wait: your success will depend not just on what you know, but on things like how you act, what you say, how you say it, and how you treat others. In the face of pressures and temptations, you will encounter situations you have not been taught about and that few people have contemplated—at least before running into them for the first time. What happens when your boss asks you to log only forty hours even though you worked fifty? When your assigned "buddy" shows you how he can get free food out of the vending machine?

When you enter the world of work, you will encounter ethical challenges you've likely never thought of, much less addressed. Without intending to, or even realizing what you're doing, you may do the wrong thing. Michigan State University's Collegiate Employment Research Institute surveyed thousands of employers in 2007 and found that unethical behavior accounted for 27 percent—the largest category—of the terminations of new college hires, with another 14 percent fired for inappropriate uses of technology.[1] Unethical behavior included dishonesty (lying on resumes, lying about time worked, misreporting expenses, etc.), theft, misuse of confidential information, fraud, and inappropriate interactions at work and with customers or clients. Technology violations included use of company equipment and networks for personal use, sharing information on social networking sites, spending too much time Web surfing, and so on.

While you might think none of this applies to you if you plan to work hard and not lie or steal at work, sometimes the choices sneak up on you, and sometimes you are put on the spot. Take the example of a young professional who didn't even realize at first what was going on when his supervisor asked him to "adjust" a date to cover up a system failure the boss was responsible for, with a reminder that evaluations were coming soon. The student wrote, "I caved, not because of the possible benefits, but because I didn't know what to do with my supervisor hovering over me. My mind went blank and I changed the date. I think about my action often, trying to decipher what went wrong." He wasn't prepared. You can be.

Learning from a mistake is the first step in recovering from it—and understanding the mistake is the first step toward learning from it. That young professional still feels tortured by that mistake, which he now understands, has learned from, and will never repeat.

> If I could rewind time and have faced my dilemma after I had taken Ethics, I would have handled things differently. As it was, my superior was right in front of me, expecting me to change the date on the spot; I already had my computer on, making it very easy to open the document, make the change, and hit print. The best way to handle a dilemma like this one would have been to have an action plan.

The choices you make in matters consequential and mundane will define you, because ethics, like life, consists of small acts done consistently over time. All too often, options do not have clear-cut boundaries. If you know in advance about possible pitfalls, and if you consider them in light of your own values and apply tools to manage them, you will not be blindsided and find yourself unable to respond in ways consistent with your long-term goals. As the young professional says, "since no one has invented the crystal ball that would reveal what ethical dilemmas we will confront so we can prepare for them, we must understand our values and practice speaking about them so we know how to act before they are tested. Now that I have experience with analyzing a dilemma and determining an ethical solution that fits me, I will know where I stand the next time, and have the words to say so."

Ethics Is Not a Luxury

You can't control the people around you, but you can control what you do. When you're caught off guard, under pressure from someone more powerful, it's easy to make a mistake. And having made one, it's easier to rationalize the next one. You can learn how to avoid many of these traps in the first place, and minimize the negative effects of the ones you land in. Ethics is not a luxury you can defer early in life and add on when you can afford to. Learning and using a few key habits can help you advance with class. Consider what you would do if faced with a few challenges like those shared with me over the years by students and colleagues:

Campus Bookstore Employee Discount

Your student loans do not cover the entire cost of college. While your parents would like to help, they just cannot do any more right now. To pay your bills, you get a job at one of the local campus bookstores. The job pays well, but you are still not making enough to cover all of your expenses. The best part of the job is that you get a 50 percent discount on all merchandise. This really helps you out, and while you won't have any money for social activities, you might break even. Early in the semester, a few classmates approach you with an offer to pay you 75 percent of the total cost if you purchase their books using your discount. If you do this, you will be able to pay your bills and have a little extra spending money. What do you do?

Do you consider this stealing? Do you see that someone else could? Both your own life situation and pressure from your friends are at play. Do you cross an ethical line if you agree? If yes, is it because you need the money? Perhaps that's just rationalizing. Would you cross the same line if you just want the money? And if you decide not to do it, how do you tell your friends?

Valet Parking

> You have a summer job working as a valet, parking cars. The parking fee is twenty dollars, which goes to the owner. You and the others are paid well through the tips that go into a common pot, which is shared among those on duty at the end of each shift. Your first day, you notice that some of the valets have a system that reuses parking tags, and for those cars, the whole parking fee goes into the pot, along with the tip. You feel uncomfortable about this, and do not know what to do. The other valets, who have been there longer than you, all accept this arrangement. This job is your best chance to save money for school next semester. Jobs are hard to come by, and it's only for the summer, anyway.

Going against established practices accepted by the senior people around you can be hard. Going along to get along is the easiest— and in this case the most lucrative—path. How do you assess the risks, both immediate and longer term, of yielding to the pressure to participate, and (not incidentally) of ceding your own sense of right and wrong to the group? If you decide not to play along, then how do you navigate what could be a tricky and uncomfortable set of working relationships?

Fare plus Five

> On your first day of work, your mentor says you should always add five dollars to the fare on your expense forms when you take a cab,

pointing out that the extra makes up for miscellaneous costs you incur but cannot document. At orientation you were told expressly that doing that would be a fireable offense—but over time you see that everyone else does it.

How do you reject advice from your assigned mentor, and on day one? Who could blame you for complying, especially when you discover that the practice of submitting "fare plus five" really is widespread? How do you reconcile the difference between the organization's announced rules and what it's like on the ground?

Assignment to Pose as a Customer

You are doing a summer internship and you're hoping for a permanent job offer. Your manager assigns you to collect information from your company's main competitors and tells you to pose as a customer to ask about their prices and warrantees, which aren't publicly available. You blurt out that this makes you uncomfortable. The manager tells you just to do it and not to be such a girl scout.

The stakes are higher here. This is not about responding to your peers or handling a suggestion from a mentor; this is about a direct order from the boss. Pressure from an authority figure is hard to resist, and even more, could mean losing your shot at a job you really want.

Double Journal Submission

You are working toward a PhD and coauthor a manuscript with your advisor. It is rejected by the best journal in your field, but after considerable delay the editor agrees to your appeal for an additional review of the paper. Your advisor, meanwhile, eager for timely publication, has already submitted it to the next-best journal. When you raise it, he refuses to tell either editor, which breaches the professional pledge against simultaneous submissions you both signed.

Not only does your advisor need the paper to beef up his own record, you also need the publication to graduate—and he holds tremendous power over whether and when you will graduate. Do you rationalize looking the other way or speak up? If so, what do you say? And to whom?

Every one of these cases is more complicated than "don't lie, cheat, or steal." Every one is a real dilemma a young professional has faced. However much you value integrity in the abstract, daily life will test it in ways you might not predict. A carefully considered and fully formed set of personal and practical ethics will help you manage yourself in the world of work.

Ethics and Compliance Are Not the Same

Is being ethical following the rules? In many cases it is, and yet we all know about rules that are dumb, or even harmful, and there can be times when it is important to take action against them.

Organizations these days are full of compliance programs, and adding to them every day. These programs aim to make sure everyone follows the same set of rules, which usually represent a minimum standard of conduct. They set a floor for acceptable behavior. Unfortunately, these programs are sometimes interchangeably called ethics programs without distinguishing what it means to comply with externally imposed rules from what it means to be guided by internal values, standards, or codes of conduct.

Just because you're following the rules doesn't make you ethical. It's possible to be compliant without being ethical and to be ethical without being compliant, though most of the time the two are consistent. At my own university, we had a lovely example of the triumph of compliance over ethics when an annual ethics test was introduced. This online test was required of all employees. It was primitive, a multiple-choice offering that posed short scenarios. Choosing the "right" answer for every question was required to pass—so long as it took more than ten minutes to complete the test. Anyone who selected all the correct answers in under ten minutes failed the test, while those entering the same answers in ten minutes or more passed. The word-of-mouth advice quickly became to start the test, go for a cup of coffee, and then finish the test. That neither makes any sense nor has anything to do with being ethical.

Even worse are the unfortunately common requirements of ethics boards governing research on human subjects for consent forms in clinical trials. These forms must be signed by patients before treatment begins and can be very long, sometimes a hundred or more pages. Yet there is powerful evidence that such long consent forms are rarely read, so their contents are completely lost upon those participating in the experimental treatments. This is surely not ethical. Regulations that can lead to counterproductive results foster workarounds, as you will see later in an example of a payroll system where the accepted solution to the broken procedures was routinely to falsify timecards.

Conversely, it is possible to be ethical without being compliant. Take running a stop sign because you are rushing someone to the hospital. That's one thing. Choosing not to follow the rules because you have decided that they're stupid or that they don't apply to you is entirely another. Some years back, I went out to lunch with an eminent scholar. He was driving and ran a stop sign on the way to the restaurant. I winced and called out "Stop sign!" Without missing a beat, he said, "Oh, don't worry, it's okay. I understand the theory."

I often tell that story to illustrate one of the patterns that leads people into trouble. Once, when I got to the punch line about understanding the theory, a person from the back of the room called out, "I'm a psychiatrist, and in my line of work, we call that sociopathy." The same drives that lead to big achievements can also lead astray. It's a big and unhealthy step to start thinking that because you are special, smart, privileged, entitled, really need it, in a hurry, or "get it," the rules are for other people. That kind of thinking opens the door to the world of why and how things go wrong, from entitlement to rationalization. It is fraught with conflicts of interest.

Choosing not to follow a set of rules should be thoughtfully and carefully chosen, as a last resort. It should involve deliberation, consultation to overcome the judgment biases and errors that creep in as we rationalize our own choices and our conflicts of interest, and a conscious decision to accept the consequences. There are times when it is the right choice: Civil rights protesters often went to jail, and worse, and their sacrifices in the name of principles of equality changed our society for the better.

If you choose to be noncompliant in the pursuit of being ethical, build safeguards into your decision making to make sure that's what you're really doing, not something more convenient or lucrative. Don't confuse being compliant with being ethical, or decide that you get to make your own rules.

Know Yourself

At the opening of most of the courses I teach, I ask students to write a few sentences about who they want to be in the world of work, specifically focusing on what they hope others will believe and say about them at the end of their careers. Most—whether they're studying law, business, science, humanities, or medicine—want to be known as honorable people, people who kept their word, who could be trusted, who left things better than they found them. This is consistent with a Gallup Foundation/Institute for Global Ethics poll showing that people all over the world, in a wide range of cultures and roles, cherish core values of honesty, freedom, responsibility, fairness, and love.[2]

But what about the people who don't value honesty? Let's start by accepting that there is probably some irreducible number of people who are just plain evil, as well as some number who are terminally narcissistic or sociopathic. Those people are beyond our reach. While they can hoodwink well-meaning, trusting people at first, in the end, they reveal themselves soon enough, so honest people can make choices about avoiding or firing them. We'll leave aside, for now, the question of whether their approach really serves these bad actors over the long haul, because we all know how amazingly effective it can be in the short term. We'll even leave aside the category of people who are like a colleague of my father's, about whom he used to say, "You can always count on George to do the selfish thing, even when it's not in his own best interest." The reality is that there are some people in whom selfishness is so ingrained that they're not likely to do the right thing, no matter what goes on around them. We can argue about what percentage of the human race has these characteristics, but it is not huge. Let's assume that if you are reading this book, you are among the vast majority of people who want to do the right thing.

But believing in these "universal" values and having a desire to do the right thing are not the whole picture: we also want to make a good living, get ahead, be recognized, and do well. An interesting study on altruism found that even seminarians, whose very calling is to do good, were prone to overlook an obvious opportunity to be altruistic, if they were feeling rushed or late to an event that might be good for their personal advancement.[3] Even those whose assigned task was to give a short presentation on the parable of the Good Samaritan were significantly less likely to stop and help a person in apparent need if they were late. We're all influenced more than we think by what's happening around us, despite our best intentions.

In the end, how you define "doing well" will determine much of what will follow in your career. Does the one who dies with the most toys win? What happens when the drive to succeed clashes with your sense of fair play? Among the many students I've asked about the reputations they want to build, one who sticks out in my memory is the young man who announced in a law school negotiation course that his aspiration was to be known as a "ruthless winner." He did seem to be on course for achieving the ruthless part, at least: by the end of the semester, there wasn't a single person who would voluntarily work with him ever again. (Note how serious a drawback this can be in a profession that requires repeated interaction with colleagues.) I've been following his career from a distance since then, and let's just say that it has had some ups and downs.

Values

Choosing who you want to be is up to you and so is whether you walk the talk that will get you there. Coming to know yourself is a critical step and preparation for all that follows. Thinking deeply about your values and being able to articulate them will help you identify potential missteps that could trap you, and avoid getting so caught up in competing for the next promotion or bonus that you sacrifice what really matters to you.

As you reflect seriously on your values and preferences, remember that you will work for, with, and over people whose values and views diverge from yours. Even when others share your beliefs and values or subscribe to the same ethical code you do, their life experiences will cause them to weigh elements differently and possibly to come to different conclusions about the same facts. Sometimes you will make big choices that might be different from those around you and that will help define your professional self, as I myself did when switching gears after finishing law school.

I'm a competitive person. I love challenges, and I don't mind hard work, all characteristics of successful lawyers. Yet awareness of those very traits brought about my decision not to pursue a "big law" job in a big city. When it got right down to it, I knew that if I followed that path, I'd risk losing myself in my drive to win. My competitive side might take over and lead to compromises that could turn me into a shark, or exactly a type of lawyer I didn't like or respect. And while I know lawyers who have managed to retain their values and personal integrity in the face of intense pressure, I also know some who haven't.

In the end, I chose a university administrative job that combined both legal and other challenges, yet—because it hadn't existed before—did not promise as clear a professional direction as big law would have. It was exactly the right trade-off for me. While it meant more uncertainty and less money, it let me shape a more balanced life than I saw higher-flying law school classmates living. It fit me and who I wanted to be.

A good way to start on the pivotal project of knowing yourself is to spend time taking values and personality inventories, which are widely available online and through career services offices; different ones raise different issues. Explore where you come down on questions about power, loyalty, competition, money, life-work balance, and trade-offs among and between them. Do you aspire to become famous? Rich? To help achieve social change? Have children? Most important, if you are not now living according to your values, when might you start, and what would be the catalyst for that?

Talk with your friends about some of the dilemmas you're reading about, and look for consistent patterns in your reactions, especially where they differ from those of other people. Closing your eyes helps you create a more extensive mental simulation of an event and picture situations in more detail; at least in one study, it had the effect of heightening ethical behavior and discouraging unethical behavior.[4] Mentally visit some of the common litmus tests that corporations and ethics courses often use to gauge how others will view situations: Would you be willing to describe your actions to your grandmother at a family dinner or to someone you respect at work? Willing to be filmed doing it and see yourself on YouTube? On the front page of a newspaper or national TV? How things look from the outside can be an important element in considering what you are willing to do.

Ask someone you trust to complete one of the inventories forecasting your answers, and compare your choices with those that person predicts for you. Does your self-perception match how you are seen by someone who knows you well? If there is a mismatch, you may need to do more thinking, because the disconnect may be an important signal for you. It's a step the wannabe "ruthless winner" might have profited from.

Because resolving conflicts of values is tough whatever the stakes, you'll be in the best position to handle such a problem if you own your values before the time when you have to apply them. Even better, take some time to write them down. Your act of commitment through writing will help anchor you in moments when you're presented with temptations in the rush of daily life.

Should the parking valet risk the summer job he needs when he discovers he's working in an environment of stealing? How far are you willing to go in saying something that's not true? Posing as a customer when you're not means you're agreeing to lie. Would you also agree to tell an elderly woman that she was defaulting on her mortgage because her payments had not been received on time when in fact they had been? Where are your personal boundaries? Where do you draw the line? If you've thought and written about your values, these lines can be easier to find and to hold.

What might seem like a one-time-only weakness or mistake might be just that. But it might have bigger consequences, in others' eyes and even in your behavior. How would you feel on discovering that having accepted and carried out an assignment that made you uneasy, your boss and others around you now think that you are comfortable saying things that are not true when it suits your advancement? After you cross the line once, it gets easier to cross it the next time. While how others see you is always important, the greatest risk could be that your choice contributes to changing you and lowering your internal bar for how you make choices and behave.

Mistakes snowball.

Quality of Daily Life

Working takes a big chunk of time and energy out of your life. If you don't like what you do, the place you do it, or the people you do it with, it can grind you down in ways that can't be measured in money. Contrary to popular belief, misery does not in fact love company and instead can lead to disconnects between how you want to contribute or develop and what really happens. Stress and unhappiness at work are correlated with health problems and lower productivity and quality of work. Robert Cialdini is a renowned psychologist who has contributed enormously to our understanding of how people make decisions and are influenced. He and his colleagues have found that "for employees who are highly skilled . . . those who were satisfied with their jobs outperformed those who were not by a margin of 25%."[5] If you don't like what you do, you're less likely to be good at it, to take pride in it, or to care about doing it right or well. And all of that can lead to shortcuts and mistakes.

Imagine yourself in different kinds of work settings. Think about places you have been particularly productive, whether at school or in other jobs. Some people are "nesters" by nature and their physical environment has powerful influences on them. For others, personal interactions matter more than setting. Where do you fall on that spectrum? If you haven't had much work experience, imagine yourself in places where friends or family have worked or that you have heard about. Start with the location (city, suburb or small town?) and move on to the office (small or large? At headquarters or a smaller branch office?). Try on different visions of your life at work: In one place or on the road? How much freedom, scope, pace? What about tone and group culture, and who your coworkers and contacts will be?

Ask yourself: Do you do better when it's loud or quiet? When you get very clear instructions or when you're told to figure it out for yourself? When the work is highly structured or unpredictable from day to day? Where people spend time socializing or where they are highly task focused? Do you like to work primarily alone, to interact with a wide range of ever-changing faces, or to work in a small and cohesive group?

Your goal is to give yourself the best chance at a life that fits you and in which you can be your best self. If you know you want to stay near your extended family, factor that in before applying to a company that typically moves people every two years.

How Much Is Enough?

Consider how the pursuit of more (money, status, power, things . . .) will shape your values and affect the choices you make going forward. There are always people who have more than you have or will ever have. And there is always another level of spending you could move up to. If money is connected to who you are and who you want to be, do you know how much is enough? If you cannot come up with a number now, will there be a way to know when you have it?

Those questions were brought home to me when I visited a law school friend some years after we had both settled into grown-up life. Unlike me, she had gone into big law. Also—very unlike me—she lived in a downtown luxury condo filled with pricey furniture and art selected by an interior decorator and had an expensive new car and closets full of designer clothes. Most of our conversation was about how unhappy she was. She and her similarly high-earning husband, also a partner at a major law firm, hated their jobs. But they still didn't feel they could make a change or leave because of the money they were making. They were living beyond their means, so they constantly worried about having enough to cover their expenses. It's an unfortunately easy trap to fall into.

Devote some serious time to thinking about happiness and money and how those interact in your life. Learn to talk about these topics with those who are important to you. Differences in attitudes about saving, spending, and controlling money figure centrally in the breakup of many relationships. Are you working solely for the money and success (however you define it), or do you want something else from life? Think in advance about how you will balance the importance of success with other parts of your life like family and community.

A feeling of entitlement to more (money, power, whatever) that grows step-by-step, incrementally, can send you places you never intended to go. Write down, now, before you get too far along in your career, a level of income at which you will have enough that you could give generously to a cause you care about, stop working full-time, or do something else that would only be possible with "enough." Put the estimate where you will see it occasionally. Use it in your financial planning as a reminder about your standards and values.

Use your image of "enough" in your thinking about what you will do for money, and why. If you end up wealthy beyond your wildest dreams, congratulate yourself, and take steps not to lose your values in the process.

One of the best things about having a moderate standard of "enough" is that it gives you an ethical cushion. You can buy yourself the emotional and practical wherewithal to resist doing something that violates your standards by saving enough money that you never feel you have to sell out. Knowing you have the option to walk away from a situation without going hungry or homeless will give you more confidence in how you approach it. Your freedom of choice can free you from coercion by people who would otherwise have power over you.

Start building a financial and ethical cushion by adopting a simple and effective habit: whenever you get a raise, immediately allocate half of it to automatic savings, and allow your standard of living to rise by only the other half. Even if the raise is small and so is your paycheck, what you can spend is still more than you had before. First use your fund to pay off your debts as soon as you can. Your savings will eventually add up to freedom. You will be able to end up as the person and professional you want to be.

The growing body of research on happiness demonstrates that money is less important to being content than we might think, though, of course, not having enough to cover basic expenses like food and rent is a path to misery. After you have a steady job, and stabilize your finances for life's essentials and some fun, how much more does it take to have "enough"?

Values Fit

Where will you thrive, and how will you know? Knowing about what matters to you is one piece of the equation. Knowing about the kind of universe you might work in—the culture of the organization and the character of prospective bosses and colleagues—is another. Unless you research the group culture and values of a company you are considering, you can end up in a setting that pushes or nudges you into becoming a person you don't want to be.

You may be protesting that this is unrealistic. When money is tight and options are few, you might feel that you don't have the luxury of choice. That doesn't mean you shouldn't think about it and strive for a good fit—and keep that effort at the forefront of your consciousness until you find the right one—so that you can protect against erosion of your values.

We are strongly affected by the conduct of others around us. Whether it's littering or stealing, we're more likely to do it if we see others doing so. When those around you are committed to ethical conduct, that's contagious; so is the reverse. Especially in an environment where you identify with those around you, because you are all working for the same company, your development will be profoundly affected by the views and values of your associates.

If you are like most professionals, especially in the early stages of your career, you will spend most of your waking hours in work-related activities, probably more time than you do with your family and friends. If you are going to hitch your reputation to the norms and behaviors of your coworkers, it only makes sense to invest in your future by putting some care into assessing them. Would you be proud to call these people your partners? Look beyond the income, status, CVs, intelligence, or honors of your prospective mentors, supervisors, collaborators, and colleagues. Consider how people treat each other and how they make their choices, too. If you make this an explicit component of your job hunting, it will help you find a good place to grow into the professional you start out to be.

Heed Your Instincts

It's vital to your future that you find a fit with your sensibilities. How can you do that? By checking the references of those you are considering just as they check yours. Do some careful online searching before you apply, especially on those to whom you would report.

When you go to an interview, chat up the assistants and other support staff to find out what they have to say about the place, its people, and its culture. (How the people at the bottom of the power curve are treated offers tremendous insights into an organization's culture.) The formal codes of an organization—the rules that show its commitment to doing the right thing—may be very different from the informal ones.

The reputation of those around you will stick to you, and, just as important, their habits and reactions will affect your way of thinking and acting. If you do not want to become a corner cutter, don't choose to work in an organization where people brag about how they game the system to win. Research indicates that "over time, an unethical corporation is likely to have employees who are disproportionately dishonest."[6] If you don't want to end up having to choose between staying in the good graces of the boss and being the kind of person you set out to be, listen for mixed messages, and if you hear them, move on. Most important, if you find yourself in an uncomfortable situation, with questions about ethics, heed your instincts. Mario Cuomo is credited with saying, "Every time I've done something that doesn't feel right, it's ended up not being right," which gets to the heart of the intuition we often have about ethically challenging moments.[7]

In addition to listening to what people talk about, pay attention to what they do not mention, especially if the topics that don't come up include things like their amazing work-life balance, how promises made in recruitment are kept, or how their boss always recognizes the quality of their work. Ask questions to get a sense of the environment, and observe people's body language. Ask: Would you come to work here again? Recommend your sister join the company? What do you like best here? Least? And, always illuminating: What happens when someone makes a mistake here?

Seek a sense of whether the work focus is on the mission or on serving the ego of the people up the ladder. Pay attention to whether the boss and others in the environment emphasize "we" or "I" when talking about the organization. This can tell you a lot about whether the environment and culture are collaborative or hierarchical and principle or personality based.

Think about yourself and your values and match what you know to the everyday atmosphere, as best you can describe it, wherever you interview. Think about how you contribute wherever you are and what it takes to do your best work. If you have to take a job that's not your dream, think about what you might learn from it to help you get a better-fitting job next time. Likewise, if you discover after you take a job that your mandated tasks don't conform with your values, consider moving on.

Video Game Reviewer

> You are a summer intern with a video game company. Your job is to write reviews of games the company makes and post them on third-party review sites. All reviews are signed, so you sign your own name. You are happy to write glowing reviews for the games you really like, because they are some of your favorites and you feel lucky to be working for the company whose products you like so much. Other, older games the company makes, though, are terrible. You don't want to sign your name to positive reviews of those games—you are well known in some gaming circles. Your manager tells you to write positive reviews of the older games, but to make up a name if your problem is having your own identity connected to the positive ratings and reviews.

You are sufficiently well known in the gaming community that you do not want people to connect you with opinions you don't hold. You value your reputation for discernment and judgment. You know that online postings last a long time and can be archived, and will continue to be associated with the name under which they were posted. However, you can rationalize your choice to use a pseudonym by figuring that others are posting under fake names all the time.

Can you justify deceiving strangers if they do not know who perpetrated the deception? Maybe you figure that everyone discounts those reviews anyway—you certainly do, and those are the rules of the game. Maybe anyone who is not smart enough to read between the lines deserves what they get?

If you do not want to be lied to, it stands to reason that you should not lie to others. You may be able to rationalize that others are lying too, but if you do, you have cheated yourself. You have degraded your trust in yourself, in others around you, and in the larger community. And all over a game you didn't like and weren't willing to recommend personally.

Would it change your views if you knew that there are federal agencies that regard a systematic practice of employees posting under false names or without revealing their company connections as fraud?[8] Would it make a difference if you knew—as you do—that it is possible to trace the reviews to the company? Should those factors make a difference? Does the likelihood of getting caught change the essence of what is being proposed?

What can you say? Drawing on your knowledge of your values, you could say something along these lines: "I am passionate about video games and I stand ready to do everything I can to help you make good games, improve the ones you have, and get recognized for them. I am worried that it could backfire for the company if people in the community learn they cannot trust me or reviews of our products."

You can think of such statements as your personal policy. One freelancer I know has such an approach, based on her concept of what is good business practice. She tells everyone who wants to hire her, "I do not sign noncompete agreements." It is her prepared wording, her personal script for this situation. Yours could be, "I only write what I'm willing to stand behind in reviews" or "I only post reviews under my real name." No discussion, no negotiation. You just state it as a fact, with a smile. Your quiet and firm statement will not often be questioned. We'll cover other possible responses later, too. If the worst happens, and you get fired, well, call it an early learning experience and find a way to talk about it and its role in shaping your values. And pick the next internship or job more carefully.

A recent university graduate went to work at a place that seemed like a great fit on the surface. She had reviewed the company's website and asked the recruiter all the right questions, but after starting, she quickly became uncomfortable and eventually decided to look for another job. What crystallized her decision to leave was when the boss flippantly asked the day and month of her birthday and plugged those meaningless numbers into a customer proposal, representing them as the result of complex calculations and projections—and having her present them to the customer. She was at the beginning of her career, and the detour, while disruptive, wasn't career-damaging for her, just a false start she soon happily corrected at a new job that she liked much better.

A student told me with pride about his middle-aged father who discovered, and acted on, a fit problem that had more serious consequences. He learned that, to win a contract extension, his company was putting together the dedicated team the client had made a condition of the deal—and was planning to disband it within three months after the extension was signed. The father quit an executive position rather than deceive a long-term client. The job he eventually found wasn't quite as high paying. His decision to sacrifice some money and career status to conduct himself honorably let him live according to his values and set an important example for his children.

If your values matter to you, sometimes they require sacrifices.

Habits (You on Autopilot)

If you travel a lot, a set of routines that you adopt and follow consistently for packing, for putting important items in designated places, and for double-checking that you have everything after you go through a security checkpoint can save you a lot of stress. If you always hold your wallet in your hand while a checkout clerk has your credit card, you're less likely to walk away without the card than if you hand over the card and put your wallet away.

Habits save your mental energy for making more important judgments. Once incorporated into your daily routine so they're second nature, habits help you succeed by making it automatic to size up and resolve problem situations. William James, the psychologist and philosopher, said, "habit simplifies the movements required to achieve a given result, makes them more accurate and diminishes fatigue. . . . For this we must make automatic and habitual, as early as possible, as many useful actions as we can."[9] Similarly, your career habits, when adopted consciously and purposefully, will help you flourish in the world of work, whether it be doing research in a laboratory, taking a job in an organization, or setting out solo.

Habits must be practiced regularly until they're on autopilot, reliable and consistent, whether others are watching or not—like hand washing for doctors. Practice is no less essential to the automatic exercise of informed judgment in difficult circumstances than it is to a physical skill like golf or shooting baskets or building muscle memory by playing scales.

Necessary though not sufficient to ensure good outcomes (again, think of hand washing for doctors), habits range from cultivating mindful patterns of thought ("don't jump to conclusions") through mastering professional tools to preempt and respond to escalating problem situations. Self-awareness and self-management embody habits of thought that give clear signals about your values and goals, read signals to detect problems and invite feedback, and set and observe sensible professional boundaries. Reinforce yourself with checks and balances to ensure that you do not skip any of these elements of good practice in the press of daily activities.

The single most important habit you can adopt is to train yourself to ask questions regularly. If you want to influence others, try to change from making assertions to asking questions.

Ask Questions

If you can master the knack of asking questions, you can use them to raise issues without contradicting or challenging those around you (especially those with more power than you have), to show respect, to give others room to back down and save face, or potent combinations of all of these. When you ask questions, you not only gain information by which to double-check your own conclusions, you show that you're a fact-driven decision maker and that you respect the roles and contributions of others.

Instead of deciding someone else has made a stupid mistake, missed a deadline, insulted you, stolen your idea, or ignored something important you were trying to contribute, first check your facts and assumptions. A former student came to visit recently and told me how he had narrowly avoided a big faux pas because he remembered to ask a question before filing a complaint. He was pretty miffed that his work had been overlooked in a highly visible submission to a higher-up, but he stopped in time to ask a quick question first: "Ashley, did my report get through to you before you sent all the responses to the division director? I notice mine wasn't included and am worried something went wrong in transmission."

His report was still sitting in his outbox because he had shut down his computer before the mail had gone out.

Use questions as a check on yourself and as a way to manage relationships. Ask questions that explore your own biases and conclusions. Think about how the situation might look from a different perspective, and ask questions of others before you form opinions. Ask yourself what might have caused the other person to act as she did. Put yourself on the other side of the situation. Could it have been a misunderstanding? Too much pressure? Even just a bad day? You will be far more effective in resolving problems at the lowest cost and with the fewest repercussions if you leave room for others to back down from mistakes gracefully. You'll experience lower quantities of stomach acid and you'll sleep better.

Here's an example of asking questions that headed off trouble.

Signing Names of Strangers:
It's the Process

You work in an office processing titles for repossessed collateral. The boss (a woman) wants you to sign male owners' names to the titles because she says she wants a man's handwriting on them.

From prior experience in the field, you believe that the signatures are not necessary for repossessing the collateral. You could just do what she asks, because you think it doesn't matter anyway. You could just stop worrying about these niceties and keep the boss happy. Besides, you are getting rewarded on volume. What's the point in being a stickler when others are doing it too?

Signing someone else's name, pretending to be that person, is a misrepresentation. Forgery, lawyers call it. Whether it is a fraudulent act is a different question. Either way, unless you are signing your initials after the other person's name, or you can find clear authorization for the procedure, signing someone else's name is not a straightforward act. The former student who told me about this dilemma asked enough questions that the boss learned that she had been mistaken about the requirements: no signature was needed for the repossessions they were performing.

In that case, having the nerve and asking questions ended up being beneficial for many, because it saved everyone time and made the office more efficient. Rather than being annoyed with my former student, ultimately, the boss was very happy that the questions had been asked, especially since the student had asked them respectfully, framed so that it was clear that he wanted the office and the boss to be protected against questions or negative repercussions. The boss had not been trying to break the law: she had misunderstood what was required to process title changes for repossessed items. The former student made the best assumption, that his boss's intent was not evil; his tone was not confrontational or scolding. It makes all the difference.

Read Signals

Before you could read, before you grasped how marks on the page contained words and ideas, they were just that—random marks. Once you have learned to read, you see words, and you process them almost automatically. They are no longer just random marks; they are signals. One of the main differences between an expert and a novice in any arena is that the expert notices and understands more, and more subtle, signals than novices do. A family road trip with my father-in-law, a retired farm assessor, brought this into sharp focus for me. As we rode by fields and pastures in full summer growth, he offered a running commentary on what various farmers were doing and which ones were better at their craft than others. He saw and understood signals. I saw dirt and plants. Having grown up in the Midwest, of course I could tell the difference between fields of beans and corn, but I had no idea whether a farmer was growing crops organically, plowing in a pattern that minimizes erosion, or conserving water. Ernie could tell those things and more. He had an expert eye. He could "read" the fields.

There is a large body of research on the differences between experts and novices. A study by the National Academy of Sciences characterizes the differences in how people learn: "experts have acquired extensive knowledge that affects what they notice and how they organize, represent, and interpret information in their environment. This, in turn, affects their abilities to remember, reason, and solve problems."[10] Experts see patterns that novices miss, and they understand and remember more in complex situations because they have a conceptual context for problems. In a study of novices and experts doing management case analyses at Lancaster University, for example, both groups spent similar amounts of time with a case. The conclusions of novices, though, tended to be formed sooner and were shallower than those of experts.[11] Expert nurses ask more questions and explore more concerns at shift change, and have a more holistic view, with pattern recognition skills for avoiding problems.[12] (Experts also practice, and practice a lot: think about top-notch free throw shooters. They don't practice a few free throws a day—they practice hundreds.)

Too many people become experts in the kind of problems that can derail careers through the famous school of hard knocks, either through their own attendance or vicariously, watching the mistakes of others. Some have great mentors who guide and advise them. Not everyone is so lucky. You can make a lot of predictable mistakes yourself, or you can learn about the things experts know and become the professional you want to be by learning about the signals of such problems. If you recognize choices that have "heed me" signals flashing around them, you'll understand, and perhaps avoid, some situations that could otherwise prove perilous to your goals and success.

"Heed me" signals don't always include enough information to make a decision—they alert you to pay attention and think about your situation. A glowing gas pump symbol on your dashboard means, "out of gas soon." "Don't Walk" means the traffic light is about to change. You might have enough gas to finish the errand you're doing or to go to work and get gas on the way home. You might look both ways and decide that, since the street is deserted, you're going to cross it anyway. You may even decide to run a red light if the emergency is dire enough. Whatever you choose once you have the information, deciding will have been a conscious process, launched by noticing and understanding the signal. If you don't know to look or how to interpret what you see, you have less information to use to make good choices.

Learning to read signals is important; so is understanding that you send signals all day long through your conduct at work and the reputation you earn. Consciously cultivate habits to match who you want to be.

Maintain Perspective

The more you can cultivate the mindset that it's not all about you, the better you'll be at managing yourself, the more your colleagues will think of you, and the less frustrated you'll be as you navigate the world of work. It's about the job, the group, the goal, the mission. They're not paying you so you can have a great car and pay off your loans and credit cards. They're paying you because they believe you are going to contribute to their mission. This applies at the start and it applies as you go on.

You might have had a great interview and might have been perfectly qualified for a position and still weren't hired. That doesn't necessarily mean that you blew it somewhere, that someone killed your chances improperly, or that you were cheated out of the job. The decision might just as easily have been about the budget, the balance of skills on the staff, or other factors you may never learn.

Once you have a job, feeling slighted, overlooked, or ignored can easily and often cascade into trouble if you don't remember that it's not all about you. If your boss doesn't immediately respond to your e-mail, or if your PhD committee takes a while to comment on your drafts, don't conclude that you're being disrespected or that your superiors hate your work. Instead, think about how much those other people are juggling. Acting on feelings of neglect can lead to bad results. If you complain, and then find out that your boss was writing you up for an award, or that his mother was hospitalized, you will feel foolish. And look it, too.

Professional decisions should be made on professional grounds. When there is not a clear right or wrong answer, everyone should know that disagreements about matters of work are not personal. The problem is that while the work might be dispassionate, people are not always. Even the most rational among us is influenced by emotion, and we all have serious cognitive biases and make predictable judgment errors that can lead us astray.

"Who's Got the Monkey?" is the title of a 1974 article published in the *Harvard Business Review*.[13] It's become one of the most reprinted articles in the journal's history and is worth searching out to read. Donald L. Wass and William Oncken Jr. describe how subordinates often transfer problems to their managers when it is the job of the worker to solve them, not pass them up the line of command. The article urges employees to be problem solvers—and managers not to accept their tasks, or "monkeys" as it takes two to complete the transfer.

Part of maintaining perspective requires that you keep track of your own monkeys and strive not to transfer them to the backs of others. It's one thing to seek advice and to brainstorm solutions, another entirely—one that makes you a less valuable asset—when your style is to identify problems and dump them on others.

Consider this next choice, reported by a former MBA student when asked to write about an ethical dilemma she faced in her career.

Do They Want You or the Info?

You have a good job and are happy in it. Out of the blue, you receive a flattering job offer from a competing company that includes a hefty raise over your current salary. You know they are interested in you because of what you have learned in your current job. Thinking back, you realize they have been sounding you out for some time about how much you know; you sense they want you to bring that information with you because they have not been able to develop it in house.

If the competing company wants to hire you to, say, produce their annual report instead of your current company's, not much proprietary information or special training is involved. The competitor has different content and is seeking your personal artistic sense and skills in presenting it in a compelling way. Yet if they want to hire you because of a highly advanced and proprietary product (software, risk matrix, customer profile, etc.) you developed, or helped develop at your firm, and both companies are in the same industry, your choice can be more complicated.

The offer stands as a direct benefit to you, with more money and more responsibility, yet jumping ship might come at a cost for your current company if it loses its competitive edge that comes from its ownership of a proprietary product you helped develop. You have a feeling of loyalty because your company really helped you, and yet you also feel you are worth more money and would like to move up. Still, it's not clear that the new company wants you as much as the knowledge you could bring with you.

This situation presents both legal and practical questions, and the terms of your contract will be important. More fundamental, though, is how you respond to your gut instinct that the competitor is seeking access to the product in a way that doesn't feel quite right. Are these people with whom you would want to work? Will they continue to value you after they get what they are seeking? Will they respect you? The answers to those questions will say much about who you become. Answering them requires you to maintain perspective about your role, to be honest with yourself, to ask the right questions, and to be able to assess accurately the nature of the information and skills you have gained on the job. How much of this is you, and how much of it is your company's information? It's a personal choice, and how you make it will both shape and define you.

CHAPTER 2

Develop a Professional Persona

Developing a professional persona—your public, work-related self—is not something to leave to chance. How you respond to stress, how you manage your time, the priorities you live by, and your reliability, relationships, and commitment (or not) to learning and growth will all get factored into how others view you. Your reputation will be formed by your actions large and small, including your reactions to life's tribulations and setbacks.

Do you want to be respected as a professional? Watch and take cues from those around you about how the most respected people behave. Your reputation requires maintaining appropriate, civil relations with everyone you have to work with, whether you like them or not.

Thinking about how you present yourself and building your relationships carefully and consciously are key to developing your personal "brand." It should spring from your choices about who you want to be—and your reputation will grow from that and reflect it directly.

Conduct Counts

Some time back, I was running late to interview a student for a research position. As I pulled into the parking lot, the fates seemed to be smiling on me, as a space near the building was open. Just as I was heading toward it, a car from the other direction zipped into it, with the driver smiling triumphantly and making a rude gesture in my direction. Ten minutes later, guess who arrived at my desk for the interview. Yup, the same guy. He recognized me and I recognized him. Perhaps because he didn't know how to bring it up, he did not say anything about our encounter. We continued through the interview. The instant another applicant with comparable qualifications emerged, he was dropped from consideration.

Was this small and petty? Was factoring in his conduct outside of his academic and work record inappropriate? Maybe his drive to "win" should have been seen as an asset. And maybe if he hadn't shown his contempt for the "losing" driver, or if he had found a way to acknowledge the awkwardness of the situation and apologize for it, the whole incident would have been forgiven. Yet he did make the gesture and he didn't apologize. Conduct can affect outcomes far beyond expectations.

Good behavior isn't just about being courteous by saying please and thank you. It is also about considering how your actions affect others. If you regularly treat all those around you, from the janitors to the top boss, with respect on a regular basis, you will develop a reputation for being a person who deserves respect as well. That could earn you a second chance after a serious mistake, let your perspective be heard when you disagree, or stimulate extra effort from a gatekeeper to solve a bureaucratic problem for you.

Formally, or informally, everyone around you is constantly forming opinions of you. The idea is to act consistently the way you'd like to be perceived by those who evaluate you. These judgments will affect your working life in ways that are not always obvious, especially at the outset. A law student I know who was well qualified but not a superstar once got a job even after he spilled a drink on the interviewer because she went back to the office talking about what good manners he had while he mopped up and how his conduct had been classy while dealing with a bad situation.

Shape your destiny by establishing yourself, from the beginning, as someone who adds value to any working group and organization, a person who influences outcomes and people in a positive way. Be alert to the culture and customs of the workplace and have the good manners to demonstrate respect for others and put them at ease. That doesn't mean being a yes-person who agrees with everything that important people say. It means that you learn constructive ways to interact and position yourself to be heard when you have a different perspective, detect a problem, or seek an opportunity.

The choices made by the student who took my parking spot affected how the selection process played out. What if you already have the job, and haven't started yet? Your manners can be tested then, too.

Dream Job, Bad Timing

> You are offered a position and you accept it. Before it begins, you learn that your dream job has opened up. What should you do? Can you honorably apply for it? Could you take it if it was offered? What do you say to the people who offered you the first job?

You gave your word, and you might have signed a contract. You have a starting date. Start by asking questions: How will this affect those on the other side of the desk at the company offering the job— one you were happy enough to get until a better offer came along? How long did they search before making you the offer? Did they have other candidates who are no longer available?

Was the search expensive and extended, or was it a rolling search? In other words, what is the opportunity cost to the company if you renege on your word or written contract? How hard will you be to replace? Is there any way to mitigate the costs to the employer?

How honest were you in the course of recruitment about your hopes and aspirations? Will the recruiter or boss who offered you the job recognize that the dream job is a better fit? What are the terms of employment? Is it at will, so you could be dismissed at any time, or is more security attached to it? The last question assesses reciprocity: how tightly bound does the contract assume each of you will be to the other?

This happened not long ago to a young professional I know. The first job he was offered was an at-will contract position. It was full time and lacked benefits. The hiring was done through an open search, seeking people for many similar positions. The start date was still some weeks off, and the cost to find another candidate was not high. A simple call to the recruiter, with a description of the more permanent, better position, was enough for the recruiter to release him and wish him well. When more time and energy had been expended, or would be, to start over, harder feelings might well result from a change of mind.

Ask questions from another perspective: how disaffected and unhappy will you be if you take the first job while wishing you had taken the other? If the employer really got to know you in the recruitment process, you were open about your aspirations, and the company would not be out a lot of time and money to find a replacement, the best route would likely be the most direct one. Explain that the new position is your dream job and why it's a better fit, and offer to do whatever is reasonable to mitigate the costs to the employer, with whom, after all, you have not yet started. Be careful as you pursue this train of thought, as it could easily help you build a rationalization for what you want to do anyway. That does not mean you should ignore it, just that you must recognize and label your self-interest and try to keep it in view. Review your conclusions with trusted others.

Use what you know about yourself and your values as you decide which way to go. Even if the search was difficult and extended and the employer turned down others after you accepted, you might still make a calculated decision to go with the dream, accepting that doing so might damage both your sense of self as an honorable professional and your reputation. If the dream job is really that, you may be willing to take that hit and turn down the original position as politely and apologetically, and with as much grace, as possible. If the opportunity is indeed ideal for you, if it works out well, and if you stay with it for the long term, eventually any stain from your choice is likely to fade. Especially if you only do it once across your entire career.

But if you turn down the job in the hand for another and that one doesn't work out, or isn't what you hoped it might be, or you set a pattern of jumping ship at the first opportunity, you may have hurt your future prospects badly. You may now be known as—and may be—a person whose word cannot be trusted.

Share Glory

Acknowledging the contributions of others can flow back helpfully more frequently than you might think. It doesn't cost anything to credit and thank the person who helped you format a report or the data center staffer who showed you how to run the numbers. That should happen in person first, of course, when you get the help, and then in front of others, whether orally or in writing, or both.

Here's an example provided by an executive I know that brings together many of these elements. Imagine you are the project leader for an important initiative at your company. Your team has made great progress and you have worked untold hours and have had to take up the slack for a couple of teammates who didn't contribute as expected. You've been asked to give a status report to the executive group. During your presentation, one of the senior VPs remarks that he's really impressed, especially with the new approach to handling delinquent payments, which has been a nagging problem for your company.

You might respond, "Yes, that innovation really excites me. It was Amanda French's idea, and George Purvis did the implementation. The feedback so far has been tremendous."

Or you might say, "Isn't it great? I'm quite proud of it, and view it as one of my biggest accomplishments on this project. We're already seeing measurable results."

Which do you choose, and why?

Here's one way to think about it: as the leader, and the one who worked the hardest of any team member, you ought to get the bulk of the credit for the good work. There's no point in diminishing that by mentioning the efforts of specific underlings. It is important that the executives leave the room focused on your talent in bringing the project to a successful conclusion, and your suitability for bigger and better assignments in the future.

On the other hand, a truly smart executive is going to give the project leader credit for the result either way. As leaders themselves, these people know that ideally, the person in charge is ultimately responsible for (and takes the credit or blame for) the success or failure of what's done on his or her watch. The enlightened executive hears the first response and thinks, "Wow, it sounds like that project leader really is a team player and knows how to get the most out of a group. The fact that he mentioned Amanda what's-her-name and the other guy says that he's not out to get all the credit; he's out to deliver the best possible result for the business. Those are leadership qualities that we want to recognize and promote."

You can think about it in a slightly different way: five years from now, when you are a senior executive listening to a status report from a project leader, which of the two reports would you rather hear?

No one is suggesting that you minimize or deny your own efforts and contributions. Being careful to acknowledge those who contributed to a project ends up making you look better than if you claim all the credit. You will come across as mature and secure rather than greedy and grasping. (People who are trusted and promoted, by the way, are usually those seen as having good judgment and being mature and secure.)

This habit can play out in interesting ways. Early in a new position I had, an administrator helped me with a problem. Apparently,

I wrote a note to thank him, and copied his boss. Then I forgot about it. Several years later, when we were each in quite different positions, a procedure emerged that required people to sign time cards that inflated their work hours, as a work-around for a wage system that set their pay rate too low for their category. I was hitting wall after wall in my efforts to get the right pay for my people without asking them to report inaccurately, and then certifying those reports by signing them myself.

In the midst of my struggle to resolve the mess, that administrator came to me and said, "Let me try to help. You were so nice when you wrote that letter and copied my boss." Despite being heavily burdened by his own work, he stepped forward and spent significant time and energy to solve my problem by helping to fix the system run amok.

I did not write the original note in the hopes of one day getting something out of it. That's not how these things work. Yet the patterns of your actions will always influence how others think about you, even more sometimes than your actual achievements. These good impressions can have real staying power.

Attitude

Do not let others define you. The only person who gets to choose your attitude is you, and your patterns of thought are within your control. Problems are always more easily solved by and around people who are positive. Emotions are contagious: The more positive an interaction, the more open people are to ideas, the more creative they can be in thinking about solutions, and the more pleasant the environment will be—for everyone.

Many of the problems and stresses in our work about which we obsess and grumble are pretty good problems to have, after all: if you have a job, have challenges, and are working on your goals, you are one of the fortunate ones. Remembering that and focusing on it in difficult times can help you reset your mood and help you become more effective at work—not to mention just plain old feeling better.

You can affect how an interaction develops if you adjust your attitude beforehand by putting a smile on your face. It turns out that the physical act of creating facial expressions affects the pathways in your brain that feed emotions. Charles Darwin first formulated this idea, now known as the facial feedback hypothesis.[1] A clever study of this principle showed that the brains of people who received Botox injections didn't show as much activity in key emotional areas when the effects of the Botox were strongest, presumably because their facial movements were so limited.[2]

Not only will simply adopting a pleasant expression help you have a better mood, your voice sounds different when you are smiling. Listeners can pick up those differences.[3]

A great teacher and lawyer whose office used to be right next to mine is a big guy who can be gruff and intimidating. I could often hear him talking when his door was open because he has a commanding voice that carries. He habitually answered his phone by saying his last name, and especially when he had been thinking or doing something else, it could come out as a bark. One day, a federal judge called and admonished him for the tone of the greeting. The judge suggested they try the call again, this time with my friend smiling before he picked up the phone. If you are a lawyer (actually, if you are just about anyone), a suggestion from a federal judge is a good one to accept. They hung up, the judge called again, and my friend said his name, this time with a smile on his face.

Because I was procrastinating from grading and heard the two calls in quick succession with the remarkably different tonal patterns, I wandered over to find out what was going on. My friend mostly manages to smile before answering his phone now, and he rerecorded his voice mail messages smiling as he spoke, too. Both make him more approachable and less intimidating, at least as conversations open. It's a good start.

Likeability Matters

To succeed in an environment shared with other human beings, as most workplaces are, you must be able to be heard by, to persuade, and to influence others. You control more of this than you might think by how you approach and think about those with whom you work. Being likeable is not about being ingratiating or a suck-up; it's about building relationships and expanding your options, especially for those times when you need to take a stand or to recover from your own mistakes.

I worked once with a wise and successful woman whose guiding rule at work was "be nice to everyone," since later on you may well encounter again those you met on the way up. She spoke from experience. She had started as an entry-level secretary and rose, over time, to a senior position with wide-reaching responsibilities. Through that process, some of those who had once been her bosses eventually came to report to her as subordinates. Just stop for a moment and guess how well that worked out for those she knew, from hard experience, to be "kiss up and kick down" managers.

Being likeable can not only smooth your way, it can help keep you out of trouble. If you feel those around you are bad people, or stupid, or beneath you, or if you adopt any of the myriad other ways of keeping a distance between yourself and others, they are going to sense that. And surprise—they won't like you in return. Leona Helmsley, the billionaire real estate developer sentenced to federal prison for tax evasion, earned her nickname, the Queen of Mean, by the way she treated everyone around her.

Her mistreatment of employees inspired some to send documentation of her tax evasion to a newspaper, triggering the legal process. At trial, her own lawyer referred to her as a "tough bitch," calling her abrasive and rude. With a different approach, she might have been more likely to avoid the tax problems that eventually sent her to jail. If she had not persisted in ignoring good advice, fewer people would have testified so freely or collaborated with a biography described by a reviewer as "scrupulously venom-ous." Her conduct in court made the jury and judge throw the book at her.

I'm not suggesting that you should be nice to people so they won't testify against you. If you commit a crime that engages fed-eral prosecutors, they will likely find pressure points to get wit-nesses to testify whether they like you or not. What I am suggesting is that if you interact in ways that build relationships, small prob-lems will resolve themselves more easily and better, and fewer will become big problems.

Create Energy

Think about the people who leave you feeling encouraged, charged up, and eager to get on with whatever the job at hand might be. Think of the people who drag you down and whom you avoid when you can. There's a name for each category: energizers and de-energizers. Rob Cross, Wayne Baker, and Andrew Parker have studied what creates energy in organizations. They report that en-ergizers are "more likely to have their ideas considered and put into action. . . . Their reputations spread quickly, and people posi-tion themselves to work for these engaging colleagues. . . . People who are strongly connected to an energizer are also better performers."[4]

Creating energy is a talent of leaders. Energizers go the extra mile—and elicit the same from others. De-energizers are the op-posite: people avoid and dread interacting with them. They can even affect people who don't deal directly with them because negative energy is so powerful—there's a rough rule of thumb that it takes five positive messages to make up for one negative one. Have you ever worked with a know-it-all or micromanager, someone who monopolizes meetings so that you don't want to at-tend when he's there, someone who finds obstacles to any solution or shoots down all possibilities? De-energizers are the Eeyores of the world.

Cultivate Your Reputation

Have you ever started using a new version of your name in a new place, maybe when switching schools or jobs? Or started using your middle name instead of your first name, or dropped a childhood nickname you felt you'd outgrown? If you've ever done this, or know anyone who has, think about how fast the new name took off among people meeting you for the first time, and how long the old name stuck with people who first knew you by it. There are some similarities between reputations and names. When you start in a new place, it's possible to introduce yourself as you would like to be known. The main difference is that a few slips back to the old name will not make everyone around you switch to it; actions that call into question your reliability or integrity are harder to recover from.

Reputations are made and shared through an accumulation of interactions large and small, and it takes a surprising amount of effort and time to change even an unwarranted first impression. People form first impressions very quickly and they are both sticky and resistant to modification. That young man who gave me the finger as he zipped into a parking space? Through that single act he put in place one piece of his reputation in my mind. As it turned out, it was the only part I ever got to know.

Reputations can also be fragile, damaged by one event or serious error in judgment: the reputation the late Joe Paterno, football coach at Penn State University, built over sixty years has for many been irreparably tarnished by the way he responded to a report of sexual abuse by a longtime assistant coach and colleague. Remember Warren Buffett's admonition, "It takes twenty years to build a reputation and five minutes to ruin it. If you think about that, you'll do things differently."[5]

Find Words to Turn Down Your Friends

You paid a lot of money for your course packets, and you know you are not supposed to copy them, but they are so expensive that it seems like extortion. Your classmates are putting pressure on you to let them copy yours. You feel guilty if you don't share, and guilty if you copy. You don't know what to do.

How much of your reticence is truly not knowing the right thing to do, and how much of it is not knowing how to avoid damaging your friendships? Would it help if you had words to describe your position that you could depend on? Like many other choices involving copyright (downloading music and videos, say), you can probably rationalize doing whatever you want to do. The copyright holder seems very far away; your one act seems fairly small and not very costly; and the chance that you'll get caught is remote. Is that the way you want to go?

If you are uncomfortable sharing your packet, then you want to be able to say so in a way that leaves your friendships intact. The more consistent you are in your standards, and the more your friends have seen you walk your talk on your values, the more easily accepted your stance will be. What you most want is for people to say, "Oh, that's a thing with him. Leave him alone."

So you might say, "I know I'm probably being overly careful about this and I'm sorry; it's just not something I'm comfortable doing." If you say that with a gentle tone and regretful smile, most people will accept it—and if you stop at that, the whole business might end right there. Less is so often more, especially in contentious situations. An appropriate response if you have acted otherwise in the past could be, "Yeah, I know I did that once, and I've felt bad ever since." Aim to build on who you mean to be.

Think about the labels people around you apply to people you know. You probably know that Samantha is always late, Jayden is terrified of public speaking. Billy is crazy about Apple products, and Reshma is always game to go dancing. You probably also have ideas about who is reliable at returning borrowed items or money, and who is not, and who you choose to avoid because you find them mean-spirited or too negative or because every conversation takes too long. Those are their reputations in your circle. You have one, too.

Privately changing the label for your conduct as you think about it does not change how others will view it if (when) it becomes known. A former student told me how he was played for a fool, at the cost of his reputation, by allowing himself to be manipulated. One of his coworkers got him to make an exception to process a reimbursement voucher without receipts, saying he had lost them. In good faith, the student did the favor and overrode the regulation requiring receipts. Later, he overheard the coworker laughing, and telling others, "All you have to do is spin a story and he'll buy it."

A serious risk to your professional brand exists in the digital realm. Bear in mind that how you present yourself in social media, e-mail, texts, and elsewhere online—which can last forever on the Internet and company servers—will be a big part of how people interpret what kind of professional you are. Since the bandwidth is so narrow, the signals you might intend are notoriously easy to misinterpret and misconstrue. Because e-mail provides no visual or tonal information (no body language to read, no affect to feel, no tonal patterns or resonance to hear), aggression spirals are more likely to occur in e-mail than in person. Don't abandon your professional persona when you go online.

From day one, your reputation will be intertwined with that of the people you work with and the company you work in. That's why it's so important that you seek the right fit, that you assess the culture of a prospective workplace and the character of your prospective colleagues. Do you want your reputation associated with an organization where misconduct is countenanced? If your boss is too creative with the sales figures for the quarter, not only could she get caught and end up without a job, you could too. If your advisor fudges data, not only could his career end, yours could wind up under a lifelong cloud as well. If a coauthor plays fast and loose by submitting a manuscript for review at more than one journal at a time and it's discovered, you could be cut off from publishing in those journals in the future.

When a scandal hits an organization, it affects people far beyond those who committed the bad acts. Think of the low-level employees and secretaries at Enron, the honorable people who lost jobs when MF Global closed, or the manufacturers of licensed clothing that carried the name of Penn State, whose sales dropped 40 percent in the weeks after the indictment of a former coach for child sexual abuse on university premises. In situations like those, there's not much you can do if you get labeled. I recall a guest speaker in our professional responsibility class one year referring to those who worked at Enron as "a bucket of weasels."

Our speaker clarified that it wasn't that it was an environment full of toxic people so much as full of people who became complicit—and everyone paid for it in the end. He told us how he had asked a former Enron staffer who attended his church about what had happened. The former staffer admitted he'd had a pretty good idea about many of the shady actions that brought the company down, and had looked the other way because he was making so much money. That guy manages a gas station now, because no one in any financial industry will hire him. And maybe they should not.

Manage Your Work Relationships

A chief operating officer once asked me for help with a line executive who was implementing all the needed changes but in a way that caused turmoil in the organization. With regret, I concluded I couldn't help because he seemed unwilling to adapt when his boss told him, "It's not the *what*, it's the *how*, Sam." Sam's self-described style was "charge on—they can get on board or out of the way." His explanation for the turmoil was that everyone else was wrong. They might well have been wrong, but soon they were being wrong without his guidance, because he was let go. He's still freelancing, because his reputation is that he's too hard on valuable staff to offset his undoubted skills, and he isn't willing to accept positions where he's not directing people. Sam doesn't manage relationships.

One of Peter Drucker's articles, "Managing Oneself," has become a *Harvard Business Review* classic. In it, Drucker advises that each of us takes responsibility for our working relationships. He suggests that whenever you start a new project, or start working with new people, you should say, "This is what I am good at. This is how I work. These are my values. This is the contribution I plan to concentrate on and the results I should be expected to deliver. . . . And what do I need to know about your strengths, how you perform, your values, and your proposed contribution?"[6]

Whether working in a small team or group or a much larger organization, how people work can be as important as what they do for achieving good outcomes. Take an outgoing person who prefers brainstorming in meetings who is working with someone who prefers careful planning and e-mail for exchanging ideas. If they do not talk about their preferences for effective interactions, here's what can happen. The introvert sends e-mails laying out ideas. The extrovert skims the notes and figures they'll talk about it at a meeting. The introvert dodges as many meetings as possible, waiting for a response so that he might lay out a plan before the next step. The brainstormer still doesn't respond, and the writer starts to feel miffed at the lack of response, which feels like disrespect. Meanwhile, the extrovert is annoyed at the slow pace of progress, because they're not meeting.

Miscommunication escalates and bad feelings accumulate, affecting the productivity of the team unless one of them has the presence of mind to tackle the issue head-on and clear the air. If you can think about and explain yourself, you'll ensure that misunderstandings don't obstruct your interactions. The goal is to end up in a situation that takes advantage of your strengths—and doesn't magnify your weaknesses.

You can extend this idea to whole companies. Consider how many corporate mergers fail. Burke and Litwin nicely define corporate culture as "how we do things around here."[7] When two cultures clash in organizations trying to come together, the results are not pretty: Sears/Kmart and AOL/Time Warner are only two examples where completely different methods of approaching problems and getting things done led to failure. It's accepted wisdom, in fact, that most mergers fail.

Students liked Drucker's idea of the three-step contribution discussion when I introduced it but didn't see how to go about adopting it. We experimented with incorporating it into all group-based assignments. Once we added a written contract to address each element for each member of the team, the group became excited and the feedback was positive. Groups reported that holding this initial conversation helped the work go more smoothly, helped them learn about each other, and was not nearly as awkward as anyone had anticipated. Try it.

If your work culture does not support this kind of interaction, you might develop your own process for articulating how you work best. If you know you thrive in interactive settings and think best in conversations, explain that; then hope to hear something back—and be prepared to learn that is not a style that works well for your colleagues. The sorts of differences we tend not to think about can undermine effectiveness in insidious ways.

Take responsibility for yourself by owning and identifying how you work. If you get used to thinking about this and behaving with this kind of transparency, it can carry over in other positive ways, too, as when you need to be able to explain why you are or are not comfortable with a proposed action that might be incompatible with your values.

Whose Money Is It?

Your team quotes a customer a price for some work, part of which you both understand will be passed through on a subcontract to another company. Your customer pays you up front for that piece of the work. When the subcontractor's bill comes to you, it's 20 percent less than you expected. What do you do? And what if the manager of your team poses that question to the whole group?

On one hand, the customer paid the up-front charge without complaint and is satisfied with the work; he will never know how much the contractor charged you, and you are, after all, in business. On the other hand, since you do not generally charge a markup in this kind of pass-through and it has not been built into the deal, returning the excess to the customer would send a strong positive signal about how you view your relationship and how you do business. At the core of this dilemma is the question of whether to take every advantage that presents itself. If the whole team agrees to keep the excess as part of its rightful fee, you know something about each other that could corrode long-term internal trust. What kind of working atmosphere would you expect in this group over time? Is choosing money over transparency and money over relationships compatible with your values? How would you want to be treated if the roles were reversed? How you define the question will affect the answer you get, so think carefully about what you ask yourself.

Manage Office Relationships

A young lawyer told me not long ago that she hated office politics so does not pay any attention to all that "feeling stuff." Big mistake. "Office politics," despite the dismissive name, refers to all the personal interactions people have at work and their history. Office politics are key in forming our assessments of each other. This doesn't mean you should become a player in power games, it means pay attention and cultivate respectful relationships. To ignore them is to ignore a very important element of any endeavor. Perhaps, in the case of this young professional, dismissing their feelings sends a message that she does not value her colleagues.

Maintaining cordial relations can be hard in fast-paced settings and with people you do not like or respect. At the same time, it's essential. If you cannot get others to cooperate with you, your work life will be tough and unpleasant. While there will always be friction and tussles large and small in any human endeavor, including and especially at work, reciprocally good relationships are key to smoothing out rather than escalating conflicts. People who make the systems work, from payroll to purchasing, are more likely to bestir themselves to go the extra mile for you if you've been polite and have acknowledged their existence before needing their help. Memorize names, listen to what's important to others, and pay attention to who is working with you and what each one cares about. Be especially soft-spoken and restrained in times of high stress. Work at it. Make these efforts habits and they will smooth your way.

Understanding what social psychologists call the sinister attribution bias illustrates the workings of a potentially toxic interactive spiral: the more you dislike a person, the more likely you are to sense cold or even hostile feelings from that person. The sinister attribution bias translates as, "I'm okay, but you're a jerk." We interpret our own actions through our intentions ("I am friendly to him") and interpret others only through their actions, not their intentions ("he doesn't even acknowledge me in the hallways, he's a haughty guy"). The more you draw negative conclusions, the more it will seep into your demeanor and the more unlikeable you seem in return.

If you have a coworker you don't like, that will color your interactions with her, and you will tend to assume the worst about her behavior. You are more likely to raise questions and talk directly to a person you know and trust to figure out whether there is a problem needing attention, while you might just report a person you dislike to your boss or the authorities and let them sort it out. When a working relationship is strong enough to resolve small problems, fewer of them will become big problems.

Personality conflicts thus complicate small problems and sometimes power their transformation into worse ones. The messiest cases I have handled over the years have always been fueled by bad chemistry among the participants. Rivals (in love, at work) who regularly denigrate each other usually read bad motives into each other's actions. This can escalate enough to lead to charges of misconduct by one against the other sufficient to catalyze an investigation. This in turn often stimulates furious countercharges by the first, and the melee grows. Sometimes there's a foundation for the original charge and sometimes not, and it's always a mess all around.

A person whose actions are under review, for example, often starts speculating about who might have reported the matter. A department manager under investigation for potential conflict of interest was cleared of the most serious wrongdoing but reprimanded for contracting for services with his wife's company without required disclosures. The investigation established that the wife's company was a large one and she wasn't the project leader, so there was an appearance of conflict but not a real one. He had failed to follow the rules that required proactive disclosure to his chain of command about a possible conflict. Even though he was cleared of the serious charge, he was terminated shortly thereafter, because he had been so sure that employee X had initiated the review by reporting him that he started ridiculing her in meetings, denying her requests to attend training sessions, and giving her poor performance reviews. Even if she had reported him, the retaliation would have been improper. As it happened, she hadn't done anything or even known about the contract. Employee Y had raised the initial question. The department manager liked employee Y, so it never occurred to him that Y might have been the source of the report.

There have been many bad situations in which the worst consequences could have been avoided if ugly feelings between people hadn't pitted them against each other and intensified their animosities. This is where managing yourself and managing your interactions intersect. Focusing on correcting errors in a positive, helpful, and nonaccusatory way, rather than blaming people, creates a reciprocity effect that will help when you (inevitably) make mistakes.

If you make it your rule to work from the assumption that something got confused instead of that someone did something bad on purpose, or out of irresponsibility or total stupidity, your generosity of spirit will build good will. (It will also turn out to be true more often than not.) Work at building relationships. Exercising the habit of asking questions, of yourself and others, before you draw conclusions or take significant actions will help you recognize and defuse potentially damaging messes at work.

To recognize and avoid problems with a coworker you dislike, put a governor on yourself. A former colleague of mine set the gold standard. He once told me, "Of course there are people in my department I like and people I do not. My goal is that no one will ever be able to tell who falls into which category by how I treat them at work." Relationships are about more than the words you use. How you say things matters, possibly as much or more than exactly what you say.

Usually, the more you know about another person, even one you don't like, the easier it will be to find a way to build a constructive relationship. A human resources official once vented to me about a manager who was trying to get an employee to quit before the end of her contract, through which he was obligated to pay her. He assigned her menial, boring tasks in an isolated room without a window, telephone, or computer. He couldn't understand why any self-respecting person with her skills wouldn't just move on. The HR person—and everyone else—knew why. The employee wasn't quitting because she had a seriously ill child covered by her benefits, and that trumped all else for her. The manager was clueless because he had never bothered to find out much about her. Eventually, he increased the indignities sufficiently that they constituted grounds for a grievance, which was quickly upheld. She ended up with another job in the organization, paid out of his budget until the end of her contract. She proved herself in that job and was kept on at its end. Many people were eager to help her, not him.

Make it your mission to consider that there might be a sympathetic reason for the conduct you most dislike. Figure out if the person has a backstory that will help you see him or her differently. Something you learn may well change your perspective and put the person and the conduct in a more sympathetic light. Even if it does not, it is your job to use your professional self to model excruciatingly correct professional behavior toward that person with two things in mind: sometimes, we have to act the way we wish we could feel; and the better you behave, the better others will perceive you.

I once learned that an unpleasant coworker had been responsible for a gruesome household accident that resulted in the death of a younger sibling when they were small. I never did come to like or respect her, but that knowledge helped me interpret some of her quirks differently and have some compassion. Her past didn't excuse how she acted, but knowing about it helped me manage my reactions better when around her. Since I didn't get to choose whether we were on a team together, nor to have input into her evaluations, adjusting my own attitude was what I had to do if I didn't want to be in turmoil at every interaction.

Act to enhance your likelihood of getting through a hard situation at the lowest cost to you. The better your behavior, the more you will be able to affect how the situation plays out. If the thing you dislike about your coworker is something that you detect long before others catch on, your good conduct and forbearance will earn you admiration, especially if you are restrained and professional until others notice the problem. If what you dislike is the result of personal or cultural choices, the sooner you can develop a way to see them in a less negative light, the easier your mandatory coexistence will be. It might never become pleasant or easy. But you will be respected for it, and you will have earned the right to feel proud of yourself. This applies to in-person contacts and applies double to online interactions.

Manage Power Differences

Is your workplace like most American ones, with an informal culture? It's not uncommon to call people several layers of management above us by their first names. Yet an egalitarian-feeling culture can be deceptive: some people still have more power than others. There are always hierarchies, even if they are not always visible. Thinking carefully about shaping appropriate professional relationships will serve you well over your career. The goal is for you to find a way to be comfortable in your own skin, to be consistent and grounded, and able to demonstrate your values in all your interactions. That means "managing up" the ladder as well as working effectively with those beside and below you. It's a balancing act. Avoid being someone who is known to be nice only to those with more power.

Even the most professional persona won't insulate you from pressure that can be applied by others above you when you are at or near the bottom of the power curve. Handling the built-in asymmetry between junior and senior colleagues is one of the challenges that must be mastered on the journey to becoming the professionals most of us aspire to be. While the asymmetry does not have to influence your personal convictions about what's right and wrong, it can't help but influence your professional choices. The power curve can be too steep to navigate without a strategic approach.

Recall the dilemma of the submission of a manuscript coauthored by a student and his advisor to a prestigious professional journal, and the advisor's decision to break with convention while a negative verdict was under appeal. He left the paper pending at the next journal on their list even after the appealed-for additional review had started. The student hated to violate the rules and make his signed affirmation of exclusive submission a lie. Committed to looking for a responsible professional approach, he drafted an e-mail to the editor of the second journal, seeking to suspend the second journal's review of the paper—and the advisor forbade him to send it, saying they should wait and see what happened.

The advisor was the senior, so his stance on the dual submission was outside the student's control. Or was it? As we'll see later, the student worked carefully and hard to preserve the relationship with his advisor while simultaneously protecting his own professional reputation.

When a superior's directive is not only unethical by your standards, as in the case of the student above, but also actually illegal, the stakes will be exponentially higher.

Charging for Work Before Authorization

Your company was just granted a multimillion-dollar contract by a government agency. You worked for two months in anticipation of getting the contract and, by law, you cannot be paid for any work done before the contract was signed. After the award is made, your boss wants you to add those hours to upcoming billing cycles spread over several months to recoup the cost of the work. This is illegal, and you know it.

Most of the incentives in this situation line up for you to do what your boss has asked: your paycheck, your favorable rating from the boss, and the natural desire to avoid conflict. Let's even add your supposition, perhaps based on strong evidence, that you are very unlikely to get caught. Does that affect what you are willing to do in the situation? Should it?

If you're not comfortable, how do you tell your boss in a straight-forward and still nonconfrontational way? You could start with a question to double-check: "Maybe I misunderstood. I remember the briefing where we were told it was illegal for us to be paid for work we did prior to the award of the contract. Did I get that wrong?" Maybe your boss will give you a direct order, in which case the fallback position is asking for the order in writing.

Or maybe he will do it himself. Or maybe he will fire you for raising the alarm.

Would you rather be fired for refusing to do an illegal act, or arrested for doing one?

Toxic Bosses or Colleagues

If you find yourself in a bad work environment with a toxic boss or colleagues, there are some resources worth knowing about beyond those in this book. Bob Sutton's book *The No Asshole Rule* is helpful to many people, not least because it might help you see your own role in any problematic situations.[8] (About 85 percent of the MBA students who read it in my Ethics and Leadership course write about their own conduct in their first reflections on the book, and executives report the same effect.)

As always in a professional setting, first review whether any aspect of your own conduct might be contributing to the problem.

This is not about blaming the victim. It's doing a reality check before you conclude that the fault lies with other people. If you find anything that you're doing that might be rewarding the conduct—or fueling the fires of conflict—that's actually good news. That means it is in your control, and either way, it is your job to address.

Beyond that, pay attention to what's going on in the larger environment. Are you the only one affected or are the effects widely experienced? Assess the larger messages in the environment. Some dysfunctional offices don't care how high achievers act so long as they bring in results. If that's where you landed, it's time to start looking for another job. Bullying is contagious and spreads when it is overlooked or, worse, rewarded. Bullying behavior takes many forms, including yelling or talking over colleagues, menacing postures, unbridled criticism, ridicule, cutting jokes, and so on. The best defense is to be sure you ask enough questions before joining an organization to determine if untamed bullies are on the loose.

Above all, do not engage a bully in his or her own game. These are people who are good at aggression, enjoy it, and are likely to have a vastly greater capacity for it than regular people do. They will probably simply escalate their behavior. If, despite your efforts, you do happen to land near a bully, Sutton's book has a lot of good advice for this too. He suggests that you develop emotional detachment and limit your exposure where you can. When you cannot avoid it, he says: "you can help protect your body and mind by reframing the abuse as something that isn't your fault and won't magically disappear—and by learning not to give a damn about those jerks."[9] Most of all, building a network of support and hanging out with "decent people" is a way to cope while considering options or resolving not to be damaged and implementing survival strategies if you simply must stay—all while staying vigilant about contributing to workplace toxicity through your own conduct. Bad conduct is contagious, and you do not want to catch it while your attention is distracted by protecting yourself from harm.

Your recipe is to seek resources (like Sutton's guidance), stay calm, enlist allies, and seek help from the supervisor or human resources. If it turns out that the organization is prepared to tolerate or reward bullies then, once again, you should be looking for a place that better matches your values. It's even better if you find a place to work that has adopted Sutton's concepts as a management ethic.

There has been some interesting research into the effects of a narcissistic boss on an organization's fortunes and workplace. In the technology industry, Arijit Chatterjee and Donald Hambrick used as proxies for CEO egos the size of their pictures in annual reports, whether they were featured alone or with a team, their prominence in press releases, the way they used language in interviews, and compensation relative to their second in command. They found that, at least in the volatile technology sector, the most narcissistic CEOs promoted "extreme and irregular company performance" because "narcissistic CEOs favor bold actions that attract attention, resulting in big wins and big losses, as well as wide swings between these extreme outcomes. . . . [They] take bold and radical actions, and engage in major strategic changes, sometimes even more than appear to be objectively called for."[10]

It's not just company performance that can be affected. Michael Maccoby has written extensively about the pros and cons of narcissistic leaders. Such leaders have star quality, have great vision, and attract followers, all of which can be good things for a place to work. At the same time, they tend to be poor listeners, sensitive to criticism, and intensely competitive. They lack empathy and display a distaste for mentoring. Maccoby's theory of productive narcissists argues that such a boss can be a positive thing—if there are enough checks and balances in the environment that the negative qualities do not come to outweigh the positives. His advice for people with such a boss: "Always empathize with your boss's feelings, but don't expect any empathy back; give your boss ideas, but always be prepared to let him take credit for them; hone your time management skills." One particular pointer: "disagree only when you can demonstrate he will benefit from a different point of view."[11] Additionally, you must be prepared to look for another job if your boss tips over into unproductive or destructive narcissism, becoming completely intolerant of any disagreement. A charismatic, visionary leader can provide an exhilarating work environment, or a nightmare one. Finding a good fit is key, as is staying attuned to whether what once fit continues to do so over time.

Set Boundaries and Keep Them

Just as good fences make good neighbors, good boundaries make successful professionals. You can be friendly with your boss and others at work without being friends. You can ask how the weekend was, if the opportunity arises. You can talk about sports or music or restaurants. You should not talk in detail about your private life. It's okay to say, "I'm having some struggles, and it won't affect my performance here," but not to say, "My boyfriend and I had this big fight and he stormed out and I drank and cried all night and I can hardly concentrate on my work today."

The power curve meets boundary issues when you are or become friends with your boss; considering how much time you spend at the office, you are likely to make friends there. In these circumstances, good boundaries are even more critical. Make it a practice to speak only of work-related issues at work and to save personal topics for other times, no matter how hard it might be to maintain that boundary. As part of your professional persona, you should be especially vigilant about not talking about coworkers with your boss in the guise of (or actually) being friends: crossing those lines can only come back to haunt you.

It gets even more complicated if someone who is already your friend becomes your boss. Make it as comfortable as possible for your friend to inhabit the boss role. The boundary will be hard for both of you to navigate, and the reality is that the responsibility for keeping your conversational topics appropriate and within the right work boundaries will fall more heavily on you. The reason is simple: you are the person with less power in the situation. No matter how friendly you are now, if something goes wrong, you are the one who is likely to pay the price of the boss's uneasiness. If a boundary is going to be crossed, let the boss-friend be the one who does it, not you.

Just about every experienced supervisor or manager has some sad story to tell about a time when he or she was obliged to fire a friend, or the sadder version, when not speaking to a friend about a brewing problem at work led to a horrible situation later. Worst of all are the circumstances when the supervisor starts to resent the friend for the whole situation and the friend loses both the job and the friendship as well.

Neglecting to tend your boundaries can get you into big trouble—job-ending trouble, if you're not careful—if you look at any form of pornography on company-owned equipment or networks. You know better than to send jokes, photos, or videos with any racy elements, right? But what do you do if you are sent stuff like that, say from a higher-up colleague or, even worse, your boss? I am frequently consulted about such situations. My response is always the same: delete the material immediately and never, never forward it using a company computer or e-mail account. By forwarding a risqué (or worse) joke or picture, you cross a line (sexual harassment, discrimination, conduct unbecoming, etc.). You likely would be violating company policy and exposing yourself to the same penalty as the higher-up who sent it to you. In a particularly unhealthy, hierarchical job, you could even be the only one who pays for the bad judgment. Granted, even if you delete the inappropriate item, the record of receiving it may still exist, but your hard drive and the transaction logs will also show that you did not send the item on and that the chain of transmission ends in your trash bin.

Even if the work environment seems relaxed and loose, it could easily change. You don't want to be someone with a trail of having actively engaged in inappropriate and unprofessional activity on your work account. Unless your corporate policies explicitly authorize personal use of computers and phones, keeping all of your communications that use a company address strictly professional is a habit that will help you. Even when such use is authorized, if you want your private life to stay private, follow the same code.

Bottom line: think of your professional self whenever you might leave any kind of record people in your workplace might stumble across—or be able to find if they go looking for it.

If you are dating someone who works for the same company, ultraprofessional behavior is crucial at work and when around colleagues. I walked into a shared office one evening to pick up something I'd forgotten, only to interrupt a carnal moment between my office mate and a coworker from down the hall. That was awkward for all of us, at the time and in the succeeding weeks and months, especially at social events when both their spouses were present.

When personal lives get messy and seep into the office, careers and reputations can suffer. This is especially true if any aspect of your relationship affects work even slightly, say if spats in the hallway spill over into meetings or reduced productivity. Do you want your boss witnessing a breakup in the office or hearing your private information become a joke at the coffee machine? If you have been too relaxed about maintaining boundaries between your personal and professional lives, one or both of you may be transferred and suffer career setback. Consider the news in recent years: the CEO of Boeing was "asked to step down" ten days after the board of directors received an anonymous tip about his relationship with another Boeing executive. The editor of the *Harvard Business Review* was forced to resign after the wife of the executive she was interviewing for an article reported that the two were having an affair. The CEO of Hewlett-Packard was fired for violating HP's standards of business conduct by falsifying expense accounts and other records to conceal a relationship with a contractor who often traveled with him. If CEOs get fired for this conduct, you can be pretty sure that it will be frowned upon for people lower in the ranks as well.

Apologizing

Apologizing for a mistake and doing all you can to correct it quickly will go a long way toward helping you recover from it. Furthermore, apologizing earns you respect, especially if you have worked on other elements of your professional self and have managed your relationships well. And a cover-up can cause more problems than the original act.

A student I'll call Travis who worked for me on a large team missed the start of work one morning without calling in advance so we could cover his duties. This was out of character for him, so I was concerned. I was more concerned when his team leader asked me to meet with him because when Travis showed up, he smelled of alcohol and gave a garbled and implausible explanation. The story he told me was hard to follow. It involved a convoluted family emergency and losing his cell phone and every other family member's phone being out of order. Neither the story nor his answers to my questions made much sense. No matter how much room I tried to give him to back down from the improbable story, Travis kept insisting it was true and even added details. A lot of people knew the true story (out drinking late the night before, overdid it, overslept . . .) so it seeped out, as these things will. By the time he and I talked again, we both knew he'd lied the first time. He was apologetic and willing to come clean about the whole mess—but by then, he'd already dug a hole for himself with me. While a mistake was forgivable, an elaborate lie was problematic.

Why? Because it's a truism that the best predictor of future conduct is past conduct. If you have lied in the past when you faced trouble, without making a serious effort to accept responsibility and change that pattern, you will be likely to do it again. If you have stolen once, it gets easier to do it again. Would you want someone working for you who was willing to lie to you to get ahead? Do you want to be that person?

In American culture, the apology most likely to be accepted will encompass the 4Rs: remorse, responsibility, rehabilitation, and recompense. If yours does not have all four components, in a way that sounds and feels sincere, it will not ring true.

Remorse says, "I'm sorry," not "I'm sorry I got caught," or the deadly nonapology, "I regret that you are upset."

Responsibility owns up to what you did and is not an attempt to minimize the problem you caused or deflect blame to others or the system: "I did it."

Rehabilitation addresses what you learned and how you will change so you will not make the same mistake again. While your statement can be short, it should be quite specific: "Here's how I'll recognize the problem, and this is exactly what I'll do differently the next time."

Recompense explains, to the extent you can, how you will make up for the problem you caused ("I'll retake the course, write a document, speak about what I learned, put in extra time over the weekend to redo the report . . .").

A complete professional apology thus sounds something like this:

I am sorry for the incomplete analysis. I failed to notice the addendum to the report and it was my responsibility to be thorough. I realize that I need to build time into my process for double-checking before I submit work to you, and that means that I need to refocus on better time management and prioritization. I have calendared every report for which I am responsible for the next three quarters and have set the deadline two days early so there is time to review it to ensure that I have included every element. I have apologized to the other team and redone the report showing their contribution accurately.

Travis was mortified by what he saw as an anomalous lapse in his own personal standard of conduct and worked hard to demonstrate his apology, along with all four Rs. His rehabilitation and recompense proposals were especially comprehensive and thoughtful. Given an otherwise stellar record, he deserved a probationary second chance. He's done well since then, and it looks like he's drawn the right message from it, and not just what he could get away with. We're still watching.

An apology or admission of error, when you're in the wrong, does not diminish you. It demonstrates that you are mature and responsible enough to take ownership of your actions or omissions. It shows that you're trustworthy and can see beyond your personal self-interest.

A colleague recently faced a situation in which she had a choice between apologizing or deflecting the blame. Working as an outside contractor for a prestigious organization, she discovered that the project liaison assigned to her was not effective or reliable. After it reached a point where the project was imperiled by the lack of staff work, the contractor raised her concerns with the organization. She was assured that the problem was understood and that the project liaison was scheduled to be disciplined—after the holidays. Finding the whole matter unpleasant and unproductive, the contractor turned to other projects, and in so doing missed all the December interim milestones for deliverables. In one of the project liaison's disciplinary meetings along the way to his dismissal, his defense was that the contractor wasn't meeting deadlines. When she was contacted for verification, it would have been easy enough (and appealing) to return the blame, pointing out all the flaws in the liaison's work over an extended period. Instead, she simply bypassed that topic (true though it was) and apologized for the lapses, presenting her plan for completing the final work on time. Her acceptance of responsibility for her part in the situation contrasted sharply with the liaison's attitude. After all, busy people miss deadlines from time to time. What mattered was the final work product. The contractor's response reassured the organization that she was on top of that and would deliver a product that would represent the organization well. Her response enhanced her reputation more than complaining about the liaison would have done. It showed her to be focused on the product, not just the process. The liaison? Terminated. Remember the wisdom of executive Mary Kay Haben: "The most important asset you will ever own or manage is your own reputation."[12]

CHAPTER 3

Why Things Go Wrong

Few people start out consciously planning the wrong act that ultimately brings them down, or expect to get caught and suffer consequences. In my experience, most people, most of the time, want to do a good job. They want their families and colleagues to be proud of them and they want to be proud of themselves. At the same time, I've spent many years investigating situations of professionals accused of various violations, which has taught me that things go wrong in predictable patterns, even for good people. Those patterns hold the key to avoiding serious problems and, even more, to taking the positive path most people seek. Some of the things that go wrong are individual mistakes and others are deeply influenced by the surrounding environment. Either way, you'll be the one held responsible for your actions, whatever factors contributed to them.

It is far easier, when hearing about someone else's serious problem, to say, "I would have done that differently," than it is to do so in the moment when you're faced with a hard choice. Cognitive biases and judgment errors in individual decision making and aspects of group dynamics affect our choices, even when we believe that we are independent actors.

Career Pitfalls

Stanley Milgram ran a series of now-classic experiments in which volunteers were told they were participating in a study on memory. Thinking they were teaching a learner some simple word pairs, the volunteers were instructed by a researcher in a white coat to flip a switch to administer a shock every time the learner (an actor, not a real subject) got the wrong answer. The shocks were not really administered, but the volunteers thought they were. They could hear the learners scream in pain. With each wrong answer, the volunteers were told to move to the next switch to deliver a higher level of shock. Each was labeled with the number of volts and a description of the level of shock given.[1]

Asked in advance about the likelihood of participants administering the strongest shocks, forty experts predicted that fewer than 1 percent would do so. In the actual experiment, though, 65 percent of volunteers kept going all the way to the most extreme level, 450 volts, past the point where the labels changed from black to bright red, and beyond a switch labeled "Danger: Severe Shock" to one labeled "XXX."

Starting at 15 volts and urged on by authority figures, participants moved in a direction few would have imagined, in the context of an accumulation of small choices. Most likely none of the volunteers would have administered the biggest shock if they had started there. Once you've administered a 45-volt shock, why stop at 60? If you've been willing to flip a switch at 150, why stop at 165?

Finding a place to stop can be hard.

The people who participated and kept increasing the shocks were not abnormal or unique: their reactions demonstrate the roots of what goes wrong in organizational cultures. Incremental small acts, directed by an authority figure (remember those white coats), led real people to cross lines. The Milgram experiments demonstrate the power of incrementalism and the power of authority; a group setting also makes going along easier in the moment and easier to rationalize later.

Danger #1: Incrementalism

Let's say you're on a golf course in a foursome with some people from work. One of the group has a run of particularly bad luck, so you all agree on a small adjustment to his score. It seems a small enough act, a courtesy even. But once you've shown yourself willing to change a number when you're with professional colleagues, you may have opened the door to other, not so small, requests down the road.

Now let's say you're asked to backdate a legal document with the golf score argument as persuasion: "It's just a number. Like when we were on the golf course." Not only did you change that score, but others knew you did, and willingly. It's a serious matter to put false dates on documents to be filed in the courts: the decision to backdate is stark and important. Yet it is "just a number." And after all, you did it before.

This exact sequence happened to a young lawyer who still remembers the sting of that moment many years later. He did not backdate the document, but it was a close call. He soon left that job, as it became increasingly uncomfortable for him, a bad fit.

Choices do not typically present themselves at the start as full-blown ethical challenges with major professional consequences. Instead they grow in small increments. The thing to keep in mind about the small breaches at the beginning is that the first step makes successive ones easier—and more likely. If you decide rolling stops are good enough and regularly roll through stop signs, you become habituated to what that feels like. It will become easier for you to skip a stop sign when it's inconvenient than it would have been before you started rolling through stops.

Not only does this change your own lines for what's okay, there's research that you're more likely to accept the unethical behavior of others if it develops slowly over time—you become habituated to increasing bad acts by others in the same step-by-step fashion.[2]

When I talk with people facing serious consequences for professional wrongdoing, those who can assess how they ended up in such trouble often relate how one small thing led to another. Few if any of the downstream acts seemed predictable or even possible from the first ever-so-small one. That step and the next ones can come from oversight, embarrassment, ambition, or from simply not knowing how to change course. Mistakes are compounded as more choices accumulate that you must explain or cover up along the way.

Is the next "adjustment" easier once you've made the first? Always.

Take lying. We all know it is wrong to lie, and yet we often lie to lubricate interactions in our daily lives. It is completely acceptable, even expected, to say, "fine" or even "great!" when someone asks how you are, even if you are not, or to tell someone in a negotiation that you are seeking a higher (or lower) price than you are willing to accept (or pay). If your grandmother lovingly knits you an itchy sweater you wouldn't wear if your life depended on it, what do you say?

While white lies may reduce friction and unnecessary pain, they can all too easily seep into other parts of your life. Telling people at work what they want to hear as opposed to what is true can become a shortcut leading to more trouble, from the convenient little fib about why you're late to how the project schedule is on time or that the fiscal quarter's numbers are strong. Taking expedient shortcuts makes it more likely that you may end up being someone you never wanted to be. Once you inflate an expense report—tell a lie and sign your name to it—you are not likely to agonize as much the next time, and you become more likely to play with other numbers elsewhere. Going the other direction, incrementalism in the practice of truth can work in your favor. The more you have a reputation for being truthful, the more self-reinforcing it will be, and the less often you will be tempted or asked to fib.

Even many white lies can be avoided. Couldn't you just tell your grandmother how pleased you are that she would spend her time making something for you, and how much it makes you feel loved?

Part of your journey is to recognize and set a standard for yourself as to what you are and are not willing to say and become. The more firmly you are connected to reality and the more you focus on being truthful to yourself and others, the easier it will be to avoid problems.

Danger #2: Rationalization

Nothing creates more blind spots in judgment than wanting a result, even when you sense the path to it is questionable. Starting to convince yourself that it is okay to do something you want that at first doesn't feel quite right can be a signal of a problem in the making. Sometimes, pressure from authority is how the process begins. Your own ambition or greed can get you there, too. Be on high alert when going against your inner voice.

Think back to the "fare plus five" directive in which you are told to add extra money to the cost of every taxi ride you list in your expenses. The warning signals in the situation are pretty clear. You're getting advice from a senior person to do something that contradicts what you were told in orientation. He is essentially telling you that the instruction you received at orientation referred only to the formal, written rules, yet life on the ground, at least as he handles it, doesn't follow them.

The senior person has helpfully provided you with a built-in rationalization for adding to the fare: you would only be helping to make up for expenses you will bear that you cannot document and yet are legitimate expenses of your job. You are owed money, or will be, so making up for it by "correcting" the numbers is okay. Recognizing the rationalization for what it is will help you acknowledge that adding to the real fare is stealing. It might not be a big theft, but theft it is, because it is not your money and you will be claiming it as your own.

There's another element at work in this scenario, too: you're removed by at least one step from the actual money because you are not taking it out of the cash drawer, you're entering it on an expense form. The psychologist Dan Ariely has done a series of elegant experiments that show that "cheating becomes much simpler when there are more steps between us and the dishonest act."[3] The distance doesn't change the fundamental act, just how we think about and rationalize the dishonesty. In other experiments, he's found that "people are more apt to be dishonest in the presence of nonmonetary objects—such as pencils and tokens—than actual money."[4] When he left cans of soft drinks and plates of dollar bills in common refrigerators in college dormitories, for example, the cans vanished while the dollar bills were not disturbed.

Even when little voices in your head are raising questions, there are always reasons you can use to persuade yourself:

> Just this once.
> If I don't, someone else will.
> It will be true soon anyway.
> The boss says I have to.
> Everyone else is doing it.
> I'll look bad if I don't.
> Rounding up is an accepted practice.
> It's only a little bit of money. No one will miss it—I'll make it up later.
> I'm not always reimbursed.
> I'm entitled. (I work so hard. There's too much pressure. They're mean . . .)

When you rationalize choices that benefit you, you can become vulnerable to pressure from people who know you have been willing to be, shall we say, elastic. The more you pull a fast one or tell a lie, the more it changes you and how you view other people. Once you start to dissemble as a way to get what you want, you are apt to become more cynical and mistrusting. If you cheat people, you assume that they might cheat you (it is what you'd do, after all), which justifies your cheating the next person, and so on. Both common sense and the research literature recognize this vicious circle effect.[5]

We change through exposure to the sensibilities of others. We do so on matters large and small, and we can change in positive or other directions. Philip Zimbardo ran an experiment at Stanford in which college students were randomly assigned to roles as either guards or prisoners. Within hours, both groups had started conforming to the roles the authority figures around them encouraged. The experiment had to be ended early because the brutality was getting completely out of hand.[6] This can happen whether you are aware of it or not.

The psychologist James W. Pennebaker does innovative and illuminating studies of what our use of language shows about us. One of his findings from studying diverse working groups, including therapists, pilots, engineers, and even the Beatles, is that the "more time we spend with other people, the more our identity becomes fused with them. We may not necessarily like or trust them but as our history becomes intertwined, we see ourselves as part of the same group." His research can track increases in group identification "day by day, month by month and year by year."[7]

The settings you join, with the authority figures they have, and the influences to which you expose yourself, all come together as powerful forces. Whether and how you change is up to you. It's not inevitable if you remain vigilant to the effects of the group and stay grounded in your own values.

Growing up in my family, I absorbed a parking ethic I call "the lobby or bust." It was considered a win to get a place as close to the door as possible. My father had no compunctions about yellow curbs, fire hydrants, and no-parking zones—and he got remarkably few tickets. He would have parked his car in a restaurant lobby if he could have gotten it through the door. We learned that was the way to do it.

When I took up with the man I eventually married, I was exposed to a different parking ethic, which involved driving to the back of every lot and hiking to the door. When I mentioned, casually, how inefficient and time consuming this was, my husband-to-be pointed out that, by parking farther away, the closer spaces would always be available for those with physical limitations, and that it was a way to get a little more exercise into every day, too. His father had for many years been on the board of a developmental services center and had inculcated in the family an awareness of their own good fortune and the importance of being thoughtful to others without those gifts. It's embarrassing to admit that this view had never even occurred to me, having been so thoroughly indoctrinated into the "lobby or bust" approach. I adopted new habits.

We like to think well of ourselves, yet both internal and external forces shape what we do in any given moment. Select organizations with leaders you respect to reinforce your best tendencies, and adopt habits that support the reputation you want to build.

Danger #3: Group Pressure

Knowing about the power of the group and knowing your own values and boundaries in advance are important tools for controlling your fate. Just as incrementalism can lead us away from our values, pressure to conform in a group can distort our choices. It can be surprisingly hard to withstand the pressure to conform, to go along, to do what everyone else is doing, to lose yourself.

Disagreeing, or even just asking difficult questions, can be hard when you are part of a group. You worry that you might be wrong, that you will look foolish, that you will be cast out. In a famous set of experiments, Solomon Asch staged groups so the subjects thought they were part of a group of volunteers, though all the others were employed by the study. Participants were asked to answer simple questions. In pretests, virtually no one got them wrong, because the questions were so simple. In the sessions, the group members, one by one, gave the same clearly wrong answer with conviction—until the lone subject, who started by giving the right answer in early rounds, eventually caved in and gave the wrong answer like the others.[8] You can watch many reenactment videos of these sessions online.

Going against the group can be hard, especially when everyone else seems sure: juries' decisions come about that way sometimes because when there's a big majority in favor of a verdict, the pressure is on to make it unanimous. This is how "groupthink" works, escalating from fear of conflict to insulation of the group from other ways of seeing things. Major public policy and corporate failures have been attributed to groupthink, from military campaigns to strategic business decisions.

Sorting out whether to dissent, and how to do so effectively, can be a serious dilemma. Knowing in advance that you might face such pressure and having techniques for getting perspective are important tools for success. There's a big difference between dissenting over unimportant stuff just to be heard and knowing when an issue rises to the level where you must find a way to speak to avoid violating your standards for integrity and truthfulness. It can be hard to find that line. There are models of resisting with grace, however. Consider the juror portrayed by Henry Fonda in the classic film *12 Angry Men* who defuses aggression and stands his ground without giving offense or losing his cool. Search it out and when you watch it, look in particular for how he asks questions and involves others in imagining different solutions rather than insisting they see the case the way he does from the beginning.

When you face pressure to deviate from what you believe, it is time to seek balance. Having explored and established your values before you are tested is critical. Max Bazerman and Ann Tenbrunsel provide a whole series of strategies in their book *Blind Spots,* based on the emerging field of behavioral ethics for helping make the choices you believe you should in the face of temptation or pressure from the group or authority; knowing your values and being able to name them, in advance, is one of the strategies that is particularly effective.

Danger #4: Pressure from Authority

Recall the summer intern who was assigned a task by her manager requiring her to misrepresent herself as a customer. Suppose you're that intern. The manager is directing you to lie. When you say lying makes you uncomfortable, his response suggests that you are naive, or worse, and carries a negative judgment. Maybe this is a perfect example of being new and not knowing enough about the environment to make an informed judgment. Maybe everyone in this business, or at least in this company, lies routinely, and you are just being idealistic and unrealistic. Do you make the calls anyway? In this case, the intern did.

In the real-life situation on which this is based, a competitor who received one of the calls figured out what was going on, found the intern's name, and reported it to her college. The competitor was planning to press charges of violation of the industry's code of conduct, a charge that, if upheld, would have prohibited that student from ever obtaining work in it.

After it was confirmed that the student had misrepresented herself in the calls, a series of very difficult meetings followed, involving the college and lawyers from both the firm that assigned the task and the competitor who was called by the intern. Eventually, the most serious allegations that would have barred the student from entering the profession were dismissed, but the professional scare and sleepless nights made for an awful summer for her—and for the professor and career services office that had helped her get the internship.

Could or should the intern have anticipated the outcome of following directions from a legitimate authority figure? As an emerging professional aspiring to work in the industry, she was found responsible for conducting herself ethically. Being willing to misrepresent herself on the telephone in a professional setting is a serious matter in that field—the fact that someone higher up told her to do didn't get her off the hook. Choices have consequences. They are not always easy to predict even if you have prepared, but preparation sure does increase the odds in your favor.

We can be influenced by circumstances and by others to take actions we would not otherwise contemplate. What do you do in the crucible of professional demands from on high that conflict with your values or comfort zone? The findings of Milgram's studies of authority and conformity are widely applicable, and authority figures can foster absolutely uncharacteristic behavior. Orders from authority figures are more likely to be resisted, however, when individuals are reminded that they, not the authority, are responsible for the harm inflicted.[9]

Orders from authority figures are difficult to resist; even people with strong character are affected by how orders are given. How the environment is structured may affect the extent to which subjects yield. The original Milgram experiments took place on a prestigious university campus in a fancy building. In later variations, compliance with the uncomfortable orders dropped when the experiments took place in less impressive settings and when the orders were given over the phone instead of in person.

It's particularly tough to resist pressure when it comes from someone you like and respect, or someone more senior than you in the organization, especially when that someone has power over you and your advancement. Besides, when supervisors are cutting corners and pressing you to follow suit, they must know what they're talking about—mustn't they?

To make the dynamic more complex, the pressure does not have to be overt. One of the keys to getting people to agree to things they would ordinarily turn down is to make a small related request first. In keeping with the principles of incrementalism, if you ask someone for a small favor and the person does it, that same person is more likely to do a larger favor later.

Signing When the Boss Says?

As the result of a recent consolidation of functions, you have become the authorized signatory for all of your division's travel reimbursement vouchers before they go on to the corporate business support center. Awkwardly for you, this includes reviewing the vouchers your boss submits. The boss recently came back from a trip abroad. His reimbursement request itemized many expenses for which there were no receipts, including a number of meals, transportation, and "meeting costs." They total more than $4,000. When you first get the voucher, you ask his assistant to provide the receipts. Her response:

"Spoke with boss. What you've got are all the receipts he has; his directions are to expedite the reimbursement because the expenses are on his personal credit card."

Your role is to certify that the vouchers comply with all divisional regulations before they are forwarded for processing. This happened to a good friend of mine, with whom I had investigated many other cases of financial irregularity—and the boss knew it.

In this case, even though you do not stand to benefit personally as the intern might have, you are still facing an ethical dilemma.

What do you do to satisfy your conscience and keep your job? We will come back to this dilemma later to explore some possibilities.

Danger #5: Pressure from the System

Not all the pressure will come from individuals. Sometimes the incentives established for performance conflict with your values, and sometimes even the stated values of the company. Sadly, this happens a lot. Here's a typical reflection from a former student who faced such a situation:

> Our customers were focused on their retirement. The products pushed by management because of their high profitability were not always the best products for those clients. My managers asked us to promote those products for higher sales income. Even though I knew that other instruments would better serve my clients, I sometimes recommended that the clients take the product promoted by my bank under pressure from my supervisors because it counted toward my performance goals and even though I knew I wasn't making objective decisions when it came to my clients' asset portfolio management.

This sort of situation is bad not just for the client and the employee, it hurts the company, too. The psychologist Robert Cialdini, who studies influence and examines how things go wrong in companies, wrote, "An organization that regularly teaches, encourages, condones or allows the use of dishonest tactics in its external dealings (that is, towards customers, clients, stockholders, suppliers, distributors, regulators and so on) will experience a set of consequences . . . surprisingly costly and particularly damaging for two reasons. First, they will be like tumors—growing, spreading and eating progressively at the organization's health and vigor. Second, they will be difficult to trace and identify via typical accounting methods as the true causes of poor productivity and profitability."[10]

A classic management article by Steven Kerr, "On the Folly of Rewarding A, While Hoping for B," illuminates these problems.[11] As an example, sports teams hope for teamwork, but they pay the highest salaries to the players who score the most individually. The pressure to succeed can be similar in the business world, and lapses in quality control are often connected directly to management pressures to ship on time, make milestones, and achieve quarterly goals. Advisors tell students to take advantage of their college years to explore areas they don't know about or aren't good at, yet scholarships may be based entirely on maintaining a high grade point average.

Reward systems speak powerfully and fundamentally to what is valued in an organization. Checking into them before you take a job can save a lot of wear and tear. If you find yourself in an organization that rewards acts that violate your personal values, you have serious choices to make.

Sorting through mixed messages is complicated, and it is a critical component of managing your career. Imagine being the young man who wrote a plea for help to an old family friend who worked in another division of the company he had just started in:

You know how much pressure we're under to sell the new product and I've been doing really well with it. A couple of weeks ago I got a complaint from my biggest customer that the product wasn't working as promised, so I went to the service department to find out what to tell him. The manager said the product is actually still under development and there's "no projected delivery date for functionality." But they want us to keep selling it because they think sometime in the next quarter or the one after they'll get it working. He told me to tell the customer that their staff just needs better training, and he also told me to slow down the pace of my interactions to buy more time. Is this really how things are done in this place?

Averting Problems in the First Place

Knowing your weaknesses and harnessing that knowledge, along with an understanding of how things go wrong, will enable you to read warning signals and preempt mistakes. Let's start with matters most under your control, your mindset.

Mindset #1: Avoid Temptation

Temptation comes from self-interest—when taking the action falls under the heading, "but I want to," whether it's using office supplies for your personal projects or reporting not-quite-accurate numbers to "earn" a bonus. A signal that temptation might be in play is when you mostly focus on what's in it for you and start minimizing and rationalizing the downside of an action.

A former MBA student experienced this in a job he had quit because he found it corroding his deeply held values, rooted in his religious faith. A high producer at a direct sales firm, he learned in upper-level meetings that the company's techniques were designed by psychologists specifically to manipulate sellers to push harder and customers to make bigger purchases. He was making good money, and yet company procedures violated his personal standards. "The more time I spent in the environment, the more I could feel that mentality starting to affect me; but I was young and stupid and had big dollar signs in front of my eyes."

Before long, his friend wanted to join the company but didn't have the cash to make the down payment on the necessary equipment. When the high producer watched his boss pressure his friend into asking a sick aunt for money, whatever had been in it for him lost its luster. He said, "It wasn't until it affected me personally through my friend that I could see everything clearly."

Create a Break for Yourself?

You take a summer internship that has been more time and more work than you were expecting, though you are learning a lot. You wish you were being paid by the hour instead of a set amount. You learn that most of the other interns have developed the habit of going shopping or taking some other break on slow days instead of coming back to the office after completing assigned tasks. You're exhausted. You could really use some breaks like that.

In this situation, you made a deal and are now feeling it wasn't a good one. Your train of thought amounts to altering the terms of the deal unilaterally. The temptation arises because you see everyone else doing what you're considering—taking work time for themselves and apparently getting away with it. Add your sense that maybe you're being exploited because you feel you're working harder for the money than you expected. You're not sure that however much you are learning is worth your fatigue level. And besides, isn't everyone else doing it? *Ding ding ding:* those are rationalizations.

Once again, you recognize signals that you should don your professional persona and use strategies to get outside your own head. How would it look to an objective outsider? Take responsibility for your actions by either living with the deal you made or trying straightforwardly to change it. If you try the latter, remember that you are a small piece of a larger puzzle for your boss. Make an appointment at a time convenient for the boss to talk about the time commitment expected for the salary you're getting. If what you're doing is more than that, can you renegotiate? Can you get released from some of the unexpectedly time-consuming parts? Opening a conversation nondefensively and professionally may provide you with information or context you don't have—and that maybe the boss doesn't either. It's possible she has not understood how time consuming some of the assignments are and will be willing to adjust the workload.

If the employer is a total exploiter, that's a different story—and you won't know if you don't explore things directly. You'll just be guessing in ways that your own blind spots and rationalization support. Don't let the temptation to help yourself by cutting corners turn into a sense of entitlement. If you made the deal, you're not entitled to change the rules by yourself.

Temptations about money present themselves in a thousand ways. Remember the valet scheme to skim some of the ticket money out of the owner's portion into the shared tip pool? It can be seductive to take a personal subsidy from office funds—from supplies, cab fares, and meals all the way to how you use your time at work and what are sometimes called "light bribes" from suppliers. When you see everyone around you shifting personal expenses to the work tab, the temptation can be strong and the rationalizations easy to construct.

A former investment banker once told me that in all her working years she'd never met a person who filed accurate expenses. She had actually been shown how to make up additional attendees to list on the travel receipts if a dinner went over the allowable limits. Then, since her office had a policy of paying for safe rides when staff worked late at night, it wasn't much of a stretch to include expensive cab rides on Friday nights to visit friends for "free."

Temptation is how a student described a reporter's offer of a very large sum for one-time access to a famous person's phone numbers, addresses, emergency contact people, and credit card charges—confidential customer information—when he found a way someone else would probably be blamed for the leak. The accountant who volunteered as PTA treasurer at her kids' school might have been a volunteer, but she still violated her professional duties when, because of her easy access to funds no one else monitored, she dipped into the PTA account to help cover a personal line of credit that had gotten out of control. She told herself it was just once but, as she told the judge at her sentencing, "It was a snowball effect." She was sentenced to jail for theft of $25,000. Crying, she said she "hardly recognized" herself.

Once you start, where do you stop?

Mindset #2: Beware Entitlement

One particular gem of wisdom in Peter Drucker's article "Managing Oneself" is his observation that many people "are contemptuous of knowledge in other areas or believe that being bright is a substitute for knowledge."[12] (Note: it isn't.) If your attitude is that being smart entitles you to shortcuts, or gives you more insight than others, it will cost you across your entire career. A full professor facing dismissal charges for incorporating (without attribution) almost an entire article by someone else into an application for federal funds once said he felt it was fine to incorporate passages from the article because "the important parts," his ideas, were his original work. It wasn't, it was plagiarism.

Remember the Queen of Mean, billionaire real estate developer Leona Helmsley? One of her former employees provided devastating evidence at her trial that summed up the pattern prosecutors were building that she felt above the law. Her housekeeper testified that she had said, "We don't pay taxes. Only the little people pay taxes." While the amounts involved and the consequences might be in different leagues, that's the same attitude that led a top leader and his wife to double order for a department party, stocking their personal bar on the company tab because they entertained so much (though not always for work) that they figured it would "even out over time." He was later publicly fired over a whole set of corruption issues.

The tax laws, just like the rules of your profession and your school or business, are for everyone—you, the boss, your colleagues, people you like, and people you do not. If your reasons or explanations for doing something start to sound like Leona Helmsley's, it's a good sign that it is time to revisit who you wanted to be when you started out.

Temptation and entitlement can be tightly intertwined. You feel overworked, so you feel entitled to take secret breaks for yourself, charge personal expenses to the company, print your church newsletters at work . . . all the way to overdoing your expense account to reward yourself for how hard you work. When you use company resources, stay within the rules. How hard you work doesn't justify what you want to do. Most companies have rules that allow you to take some time here and there to send personal messages or make personal calls, at least in part because they realize that it reduces distraction and certain calls just have to be made during the workday, like scheduling a doctor's appointment. It can increase productivity to allow people to take care of things like that rather than requiring them to leave work or clock out.

Computer use falls into a whole different category for both temptation and entitlement—and the likelihood and consequences for violations. Remember that, no matter how private it might feel when you're web-surfing by yourself at your computer, employers have the right to look at all your company-related files and e-mail and track your destinations just as they control your use of their resources, from networks to company equipment, from scanners to telephones to cars.

If you can internalize that the rules are for everyone, and that even your greatest desires don't make it okay to break rules when it suits you, you will have learned one of the most important lessons of safeguarding your core values and your reputation.

Mindset #3: Temper Ambition

Ambition arises when you think an act will help you look better to your boss or otherwise advance your career, image, or finances. Like entitlement, ambition is often intertwined with temptation, as the temptation exists in part because of the ambition. Telling them apart is not as critical as knowing that either one, or both in combination, can lead you far from your original goals for your career.

A longtime dean of admissions at MIT published a very successful book during her tenure there. In it she wrote, "Holding integrity is sometimes very hard to do because the temptation may be to cheat or cut corners. . . . But just remember that 'what goes around comes around,' meaning that life has a funny way of giving back what you put out."[13]

Her life took one of those turns when the school got an anonymous call about her credentials. Upon investigating, her bosses learned that her résumé listed degrees she did not have. When resigning, she said, "I misrepresented my academic degrees when I first applied to work here twenty-eight years ago and did not have the courage to correct my résumé when I applied for my current job or at any time since."[14]

Ouch.

The dean compounded her first mistake—listing a degree she hadn't earned—when she never came clean or corrected it, and she doubled down by adding more unearned degrees as she went along to make her credentials look even better. The longer it went on, the harder it got to correct. You can be pretty sure she never dreamed she would end up as the dean of admissions when she made that first false claim, though you do wonder how she managed to forget about her résumé lapses when writing about integrity.

Résumé embellishment can be a major source of career disaster, from not getting the job in the first place to dismissal once it's discovered. It happens to students hoping to get their foot in the door for an interview by slightly inflating their grade point averages and it happens to CEOs and CFOs, in the private and public sectors. If the credentials you submit when you apply for the job are not accurate, you'll have no recourse when you're fired. Remember the Notre Dame head football coach who only lasted five days after a background check showed his credentials had been falsified? The CEO of Radio Shack who was fired for claiming degrees from a school that never had such a program? The Yahoo CEO who claimed one degree he had and one he did not, and then tried to blame a headhunter for the misstatement on his resume? Or the Homeland Security official whose "degree" turned out to be purchased from a diploma mill? A quick online search will yield you plenty of recent victims of their own ambition.

The zeal to succeed can be more subtle, too. A former student told me about pouring energy into a presentation for weeks, even as she and her teammates became increasingly nervous about the validity of some of the numbers they were getting from the client. It wasn't until a preliminary project review that her upper management pulled the plug, saying they weren't going to risk their company's reputation for integrity with the questionable data. She'd been so close to the effort and desire to show that her team could deliver that she'd lost lost track of how far out on a limb the shaky facts were taking them.

It's your job to keep track of where your actions are leading. Don't lose sight of the forest for the trees.

Mindset #4: Face Embarrassment

> You made a mistake in overseeing a project, and extra work had to be done to correct for your error. The company that did the added work forgot to bill for it. You didn't notice right away, but later you recognized the error and also realized that, if you kept quiet, maybe no one would discover your carelessness.

It is appealing to keep quiet. Speaking up can be inconvenient, uncomfortable, and, possibly, much worse. Fixing significant mistakes may well cause disruption, discomfort, and expense and make a lot of people look bad, starting and ending with you. What if you just keep quiet?

One of the first rules of being in a hole is to stop digging. When you make a mistake, trying to avoid embarrassment by covering it up can get you into serious trouble—more than the original misstep. Martha Stewart went to prison for lying to federal investigators, not for the insider trading they were investigating.

The choices we make when we're embarrassed include those that stem from not knowing how to say, "I don't know" or "I made a mistake." It's not just in the moment that embarrassment causes problems; it is in being unwilling or unable to go back afterward to say, "Oops, something is wrong." In the medical arena, there is accumulating evidence that forthright acknowledgment of and apology for even serious mistakes reduces the rate at which doctors and hospitals are sued for malpractice. In one study, 20 percent of parents who sued after a baby died during delivery told the researchers, "the only reason we ever filed suit is that nobody would ever tell us what happened."[15] Back to the admissions dean: however embarrassing it would have been for the dean to come clean early on pales in comparison to how much harder it became with each move to increasingly responsible positions. (Ironically, the entry-level job she had embellished her resume for? It didn't require the degree she had made up.)

The signals for embarrassment are internal. You should know how the different forms feel. It's part of self-knowledge to be able to label it for what it is and face up to it, especially at work. When you recognize the signals of flinching from the truth because you might look bad, you will be surprised at how much respect you can earn by saying, "I don't know the answer to that. I'll find out and get back to you," or "I'm not prepared today."

Mindset #5: Conquer Irresponsibility

Inattention or laziness are when you know better and still don't exert yourself to do a job properly—like recording the source of ideas you write down, or when you don't correct something you know is not quite up to standards, or when it's just easier to go along than to take on the work of doing a task in the most responsible way.

The CEO of Raytheon published a booklet on management that landed him on the cover of a business magazine with the headline "The C.E.O.'s Secret Handbook."[16] He said he had collected lessons he had scribbled down over the years on scraps of paper and that had guided his work. The company gave away hundreds of thousands of copies of his *Swanson's Unwritten Rules of Management*. In the preface he wrote, "In Rule No. 10, I urge you to be sure to share the credit. . . . I happily do so here and now. This is really a product of experiences over the better part of a lifetime, of people I have learned from, the things I have heard and read."

There was only one little problem: more than half of the rules turned out to be identical, word for word, to those in an earlier book, *The Unwritten Laws of Engineering*, by W. J. King, a UCLA engineering professor. Others were copied verbatim from former secretary of defense Donald Rumsfeld and one even closely tracked an observation by the humor writer Dave Barry. The CEO had used the rules, talked about them, thought about them, and illustrated them with his own stories across his career. Each time he told a story or illustrated one of Professor King's rules with an experience of his own, the more it felt like his original idea. In the process, he lost track of their origin. Oops.[17]

Maybe his first small step was expedient or careless—not noting whose idea it was when he wrote down a rule that appealed to him on one of his little scraps of paper. He might have been more careful if he had known himself well enough to recognize that he might forget where he had first come across the ideas, or if he was sufficiently self-aware to realize that he was incorporating them as his own.

People who do their jobs mindlessly, more focused on the paycheck than the work or its consequences, are not owning responsibility for their work. Often, people who got into real trouble because of laziness knew full well they were opting to ignore signs of problems to make their own lives easier: they say that doing anything when someone was seriously violating safety or financial regulations just seemed like more trouble than it was worth—or they say they felt so much pressure to make deadlines that they just skipped a step or two in the process.

That assessment changes, of course, when facing consequences for being an accessory or coconspirator, and it is often too late by then. A series of skimped quality control tests in the manufacture of dialysis supplies once killed thirteen people. Lockheed Martin has a video illustrating a similar kind of problem in its ethics series called "Integrity Minute" that shows the consequences of one employee rationalizing skipping a step in the quality control process because, she reassured herself, others would be checking it later anyway. In that case, a combination of laziness, inattention, and ambition cost the company a customer, public embarrassment, and fines, and cost the employee career advancement.

Speak Up or Keep Quiet?

You are put in charge of handling accounts payable, and you discover your company has underpaid royalties by a million dollars. The person in charge at that time is now your boss. If you bring this to light, it will cost your company money, you will look bad, your own budget will take the hit, and you will be making your boss look bad, too. Nobody has noticed the mistake for all these years. It's really tempting to keep ignoring it. That would be so much easier.

Keeping quiet is the expedient course. But if you can find a professional way to go about correcting the errors and find the words to use while doing it, you might be more comfortable doing the right thing.

Start with the hardest case: your boss is the one who made the error. Hands down your best bet is to make it possible for your boss to discover the problem and bring it to light, and thereby play the honorable role of self-reporter and corrector. Take records to your boss that make the discrepancy obvious, and ask questions—say that you might have misunderstood the situation, which you might have. You will give her the room to manage the situation to her benefit and allow her to come to the conclusion about the error in the most face-saving way. Although she may be smarting over the mistake (and over having an underling point it out), with a little luck and the right personality, she will step forward and solve the problem.

At the other end of the luck spectrum, your boss will be touchy about mistakes and likely to blame others, or, worse, will direct you to cover it up. Your course of action will need more thought and finesse. Working backward, it's worth thinking about what you will say and how you will say it if or when the situation is discovered. If you wouldn't like it if others found out that you overlooked the error (either by commission or omission), what does that tell you?

Willingness to do something only if it stays concealed is not a good sign. While it's far more comfortable not to call attention to a mistake, a forthright apology can be the best possible response to a problem. That's true even when the mistake is a costly one, and maybe even especially then. A costly mistake is likely to grow over time.

A side comment: being lazy is different—you know how it feels—from making a conscious decision that a job is "good enough" for a given purpose. The perfect can be the enemy of the good, as when you delay finishing something for so long to make it "just a little bit better" that the entire purpose of the project is lost. For many routine tasks, a 7 or 8 on a scale of 10, done today, is better than a 10 a week or two later. Choosing the 7 over the 10 for a job where the 7 suffices is not necessarily laziness; it can be a smart allocation of resources. Obviously, this is not the case where precision and accuracy are paramount, and knowing the difference between which jobs require the 10 every time and those for which a fast 7 or 8 will keep things moving is a key career skill.

Mindset #6: Don't Fool Yourself

A young man, put in charge of purchasing for his company, was pressured by his mother and sister to buy from his nephew's startup to help it get established. Confident that he would be able to evaluate the quality of his nephew's products and do right by his own company while at the same time doing a good thing for his family, he ordered from the startup. What his confidence obscured, however, was how the nephew inflated prices and cut corners. Because he knew what an important customer he was for the startup, and because every time there was a problem he solved it—or so he thought—his misplaced confidence trumped his judgment of his actions and their consequences for his own company, and he explained away the compromises he was making. In retrospect, he learned that he'd been blinded by his overconfident belief that he would know, and never cross, the boundary of problem conduct.

Focusing on his good intentions rather than on the effects of his choices, he gave himself more credit than he should have and didn't examine the situation from other points of view. This eventually cost him dearly.

This disconnect, sometimes called the intent-effect dichotomy, also shows up frequently in office disputes where one person's conduct deeply offends another, though the first person never intended to hurt the feelings of the second.

For reasons of self-esteem and self-interest, most of us tend to think better than we should of our knowledge, moral character, and the accuracy of our own self-assessments. Extensive research on self-deception tells us we are vulnerable to error in multiple dimensions.

One of the obstacles to seeing our own shortcomings clearly is called the "above average" effect. While we all need optimism to let us take on challenges, there are real limits to what is healthy or sensible to believe about our own abilities. For example, in a survey by the College Board of over one million college students in 1976–1977, 60 percent rated themselves above average in athletic ability compared to their peers and 70 percent rated themselves above average in leadership ability. My favorite finding is that 25 percent rated their own skills in the top 1 percent.[18] It is not just young people who are susceptible to this cognitive error. Another study that year showed that 94 percent of college professors thought themselves above average.[19] These results have been replicated with perceptions of driving skill, ethics, intelligence, happiness, attendance at work . . . you name it. We tend to think we are better than we are at tasks we do frequently.

Research on the differences between novices and experts demonstrates that the less novices know about an area, the more likely they are to overestimate their competence.[20] When you think about it, it makes sense. You need to know a fair amount about something to assess it accurately. The less you know, the harder it is to make a truly informed judgment.

There's one other element of self-deception that is important to understand: because of our drive to think well of ourselves, cognitive dissonance can set in when we violate our own standards. We start to normalize the conduct. A sad example of this showed up in a long *New York Times* profile of an Olympic boxer whose father had gone to prison for abusing her and her sister. "The counselors in prison made him aware of how the mind creates justifications to tolerate its own misdeeds. 'When you do things for a long time that you know to be wrong, you come to think that it's right.' "[21]

The more you are aware of the pitfalls of self-deception, the more you can guard against them.

Mindset #7: Check Conflicts of Interest

> Working as an executive secretary, I had to choose whether to finish an important project on time or attend a series of events that was important to my personal future. If I finished the project on time, I would miss the events, which would not be offered again soon. If I went to the events, then the project would be delayed.

Whenever company resources, including your time, might be applied to something that benefits you or your family outside the terms of your employment contract, you face a conflict of interest. Conflicts large and small come up all the time, from doing your side job on company time to using office equipment to produce your annual Christmas letter.

Doctors who buy expensive diagnostic equipment and then have an incentive to order patient tests that use it face conflicts of interest. So do college professors who assign their own books as required texts for their students. Approaching customers on your corporate mailing list for any reason outside your job should be a red flag, and so should use of other company information or resources. Unless there's a clear policy that permits what you're contemplating, be careful. Some conflicts of interest can be mitigated—say if the college professor doesn't get royalties from assigning her own textbook, or donates them to the college to benefit students—while others cannot. Either way, the only way to be safe in such situations is that the conflicts must be disclosed, approved (or not), and over-seen by objective others.

Overlooking your own conflicts happens most often when you have convinced yourself that you're acting for the good: the execu-tive who hired his girlfriend for a consulting position requiring her to travel with him, justified it on the grounds that her skills were special and were benefiting the company. To steer clear of conflicts of interest, you will need good boundaries, sensitivity to "heed me" signals, and a habit of seeking advice to get outside your own head and see how your actions might look externally.

A young fund-raising professional described feeling uncomfort-able when an older donor began saying things like, "Well, I sure wish you were my daughter. You're nicer to me than she is. . . ." Occasionally, those feelings spilled over into actions, and the donor would want to give the development officer gifts or even name her in the couple's wills. Where is the line? If the gift has only symbolic significance without great monetary value, would it be appropriate for the fund-raiser to accept it, given that her job, after all, is to cultivate relationships on behalf of her organization? The decision-making framework we'll cover in the next chapter will help you, not only to identify the rules and ethical constraints of the situation, but also to locate resources to find and operate within appropriate professional boundaries.

Frequent Flyer Miles

> For your latest trip, the travel office has sent you an airline itinerary at a really low fare for your approval. You prefer a different airline because it earns you frequent flyer miles. Should you approve the travel office itinerary or take a little time, do the legwork on your own, and find as close a fare as you can that earns you miles?

Your personal preference for a specific airline creates a conflict of interest because spending the company's money creates a personal benefit. You can rationalize this by thinking nobody cares. It's within the slack in the budget. It's no big deal. Does your corporation have a policy about frequent flyer miles? Do you know what it is? Does the travel office inquire about personal preferences, or is there a corporate policy about which airlines to fly? Frequent flyer miles may be seen as a perk for the traveler, or they may be seen as company property if earned on company business. You should be especially sensitive to your organization's culture and norms about expense accounts and perks, because they can trip up young (and old) professionals, and standards vary wildly from one workplace to another.

If your company doesn't care, this whole matter is easily resolved. You can go to your travel office or your boss and say, "the tickets are ballpark the same price, and I earn miles with this airline, so I'd rather fly them. Is that okay?" If the answer is yes, you're set.

If they say no, you (now better informed) will have to be thinking about your next step.

What if your corporate headquarters has made a deal with a preferred air carrier for significant reductions in fares? No trips at those fares earn frequent flyer miles.

Then you might be costing the company money. If you buy your airplane tickets on your personal credit card and submit the tickets for reimbursement, you might be able to rationalize a little more and figure that using the free miles for family trips goes toward balancing the fact that your work travel takes you away from home so much. If you stick with your transparency policy, tell your boss your plan, and he approves it, you're golden. If he says no, at least you haven't done it and been caught, with whatever penalties might apply.

If you do not want to ask because you fear the answer will be no, or because you've heard the Machiavellian advice that it's easier to ask for forgiveness than permission, that's probably a signal to heed. Whatever you do will be setting you on a path in your own working style and in how others perceive you.

A variation of this dilemma that comes up regularly is the proposal that, because you save the company money in some other arena (say you get hotels cheaper than the corporate rate by using an online hotel bidding system), you'll be okay "trading" those savings for your frequent flyer miles. Now you're deep into rationalization. Still, all of this might be completely fine with your company if you apply a policy of transparency. Ask: "Is it okay if I pull this swap, stay within budget, and do something that pleases my family, too?" Simple, if you get permission and it's on the record. What if you get a mixed message from your boss, though? "Sure, so long as you don't get caught. If you do, I'll have to say I didn't know and didn't approve it." This is all getting pretty complicated over a small-dollar item, isn't it? Easier still is to avoid the conflict entirely by devising and adhering to personal-work boundaries from the start of your career.

The answers are not always directly in your control. Pressure to hire relatives of important clients or to overlook problems they cause can be intense:

> The son of our most important client got a job at our company, working for one of the other VPs. When the other VP left for a new job, I inherited him at a time when we were downsizing and letting good people go. He did pretty much whatever he wanted and refused assignments he thought were boring or beneath him, which meant he didn't do much of anything. Keeping him in our group while the work was piling up and some really strong performers were being terminated just didn't feel right to me, but the message came through that I should do whatever it took for him to stay happy.

Someone above you on the food chain has decided that it's best for the overall business to keep the son. Are there things you can do without damaging your own career? Can you decide the bigger picture is above your pay grade and let it go, or find ways to engage the son so he's not so much dead weight in your group? You have an obligation to the morale of other employees, too.

Resolution to the Purchasing Agent with
the Conflict of Interest
The young purchasing agent who bought from his nephew's startup overconfident about his capacity to do right by his family and his

employer did not realize how he and his company would look to outsiders. They saw the situation as a serious conflict of interest, and as self-dealing besides, even though he himself wasn't making any money from the nephew's enterprise. He got fired for it. (It's worth noting that there's a cultural norms aspect to the boundaries in this situation. There are affiliation cultures in which dealing with a family member would not be seen as a violation, and might even be expected. Knowing the rules you're playing by is always important.) It was an expensive lesson, and he was able to learn from the experience. When he got a second chance in another industry, he cultivated mentors and a set of habits to help him avoid blind spots going forward.

With good habits, you can avoid problems in the first place and minimize the impact of those you do not manage to avoid. Learn to be wary of the dangers in this chapter and adopt the mindsets to protect against the vulnerabilities, which after all, you share with most other people. Your self-awareness will help you anticipate and avoid problems. We'll add some powerful tools for dealing with the issues that still come your way so you can maximize your ability to handle them, and well.

CHAPTER 4

How Things Go Right

You don't just want to ensure that things don't go wrong. That's pretty dismal. Both your happiness and success depend on making them go right. Mastering a structured approach to decision making, constructing personal scripts, and using a powerful technique called the And Stance gives you three tools you can rely on for getting things right. If you learn, practice, and make habits of them, you will be able to avert or troubleshoot problem situations, both the predictable ones and the other more troublesome ones.

Analytical Decision Making

Have you ever had a great teacher who asked such good questions that you could figure out the answers for yourself? Your goal is to become that person. The way to get there is to use a structured, analytical, decision-making framework to help you overcome your inexperience and avoid judgment errors in the face of uncertain choices. If you can practice using the decision-making framework until it becomes an automatic response at choice points—almost a reflex action—you will more expertly understand the situations in which you find yourself. This approach will help you develop strong responses that support and advance your professional goals.

There is nothing magical about the questions in the framework used here. You will likely encounter other versions in your career. Most large corporations with ethics programs have one, though the exact content will vary. What will not change is the idea that consistently using a structured analytical approach will aid you in making a quick and reasonably comprehensive assessment of your options, set within a larger framework of values and goals.

- Identify the issues.
- Inventory the rules and regulations that apply.
- Broaden your perspective by asking questions.
- Assess resources available to help you.
- Review options and who is affected by each.

Depending on the choice you face, some of the steps in the framework will be more important than others. Don't skip any, though, as systematically addressing each one, every time, will build your decision-making "muscle." Remember the research described in Chapter 1 about its beneficial effects, and close your eyes when you are working your way through them, to maximize your effective use of the tool.

Revisiting Fare plus Five

Think back to the dilemma about the advice to pad your expenses by five dollars when you submit cab fares. Begin by identifying the issues:

- Mixed messages: your orientation versus life on the ground as everyone seems to live it
- Financial temptation
- The awkwardness of ignoring advice from assigned mentor
- Lying about the amount of the fare (stealing) by falsely claiming expenses

You may see other issues in the situation, once you stop to think about it. For the ones you've already spotted, review what the rules and regulations say about each.

Inventorying Applicable Rules and Regulations

You already know from your orientation that false claims on an expense report are a fireable offense. You may also know that expense reports are among the most frequently audited aspects of internal controls in a corporation. (If you didn't know that, you do now.) Among other rules that apply, although they might not come to mind so quickly:

- Your company's code of conduct;
- Your profession's code of ethics if it has one;
- Your personal code: are you comfortable signing your name to a lie?

Asking Questions

What questions should you ask? The ultimate one is how the decision represents who you want to be by the end of your career. Others that might come to mind:

- Will your mentor see your expense reports and find out if you don't follow his advice?
- What will you say if caught? To your mentor? To your supervisor? (How persuasive will it be if you say, "My mentor told me to do it," when your orientation specifically addressed this as a fireable offense?) How will you feel and what will you tell people if this becomes public?
- Do people really get fired for this at your company? How likely is it that you will get caught?
- Is this a one-time thing or are you going to face this choice often?
- The litmus tests: How will you feel if your choice ends up in the news, or if your most respected mentor finds out what you did?

• What does the employee handbook say? Did you sign something indicating you understood and accepted the company's regulations?

Assembling Resources

Assess the resources that are available to you to help answer the questions and work your way through the dilemma:

• Your own sense of what is right and wrong
• Your upbringing
• The people you respect and trust
• A company hotline
• The person who recruited you to the job
• The person who ran your orientation
• The handbook they gave you
• The lessons of misconduct this book explores

Defining Options and Identifying Who
Will Be Affected by Each

• Report more than you paid on your expense report
• Report only what you paid

You are the one most likely to be affected, though so will the company budget, in the long run. Who you are and what you want to stand for are at stake.

And now it's time to decide.

Each choice has implications to think through. If you're not going to add to your actual fare, are you going to say anything about the advice you received, or just keep quiet? Are you going to report the situation, even in a low-key way by asking questions? You'll need to come up with the words you'll use, either way. Can you trust the other advice you get from this mentor?

The temptation is to add "just a little bit" to your fares here and there, to make up for other expenses that will be out-of-pocket because you won't have documentation. And perhaps it does seem that "everyone does it that way." Pause and think, even if just for a moment, about the other way to frame this situation: you are contemplating stealing money and signing your name to a lie. For five dollars. Would you take five dollars off someone's desk at work? Would you take five dollars out of a wallet? Would you take five dollars out of the coffee fund to pay for your lunch? Would you do any of that if someone was watching? The only difference here is that you'd be taking the money through paperwork rather than by hands-on theft. The five dollars is not yours.

Padding your expense account is the top of that proverbial slippery slope. Maybe you'll never get caught and you'll be "richer" for it by a few hundred dollars here and there. The "only" cost then is how you feel about yourself and how others perceive you. Maybe in that company, they'll even see you as more of a player if you are going along to get along. Maybe, though, others might notice that your mentor is a little loose with following rules, and may be observing how you react and may assess you on that basis; you might never know.

Fare plus Five Resolved

The young professional who had this experience chose not to embellish his expenses and watched, over the next year, as his assigned mentor came under closer and closer scrutiny and then was quietly asked to leave the firm. If that young man, now a top executive with the company, which prides itself on its ethical culture, had taken his mentor's advice, his career might have had a very different trajectory.

In many situations, the most obvious question is whether you're willing to deal with the repercussions if you're caught doing whatever it is that's making you think twice. Equally important to consider is how the choice might affect your thinking and accumulate over time.

Revisiting the Valet Parking Dilemma

The new valet whose coworkers expected him to go along with their scam to pocket some of the ticket fees had decisions to make in Chapter 1. Applying the structured decision-making process to the quandary he faced, students often define the issues as getting along with coworkers and whistle-blowing. Those are important issues to consider—as far as they go. Yet, they leave out another: again, the fundamental issue here is theft. The legal definition of theft is taking the property of another person without permission and with the intent to keep it. Does that money belong to the valets? No. It belongs to the owner. Is the owner permanently deprived of it? Is that the intent of this entire system of reusing parking tags? Yup.

When we focus on the valet's options in light of the huge difficulties in doing anything about the system in place, students often adopt the argument that it's only for the summer and it's not very much money—between $500 and $1,000 for the least senior valet. And he's still at the top of the same slippery slope as the fellow with the fare-plus-five dilemma: would you steal $1,000 from the owner if it was lying on the table and you were sure you wouldn't get caught? How about $1,500 or $5,000? A million? What if you knew taking the money might be videotaped? No matter what, would you steal at any level? Or do you draw a line at at certain amount? Where? How?

Accurately identifying the underlying issue as it appears to those not personally involved or benefiting can help you avoid the trap of rationalizing away acts that could get you fired, or arrested, or otherwise tarnish your name. Knowing that it's important to try to counteract your own rationalizations and cognitive biases, actively seek perspectives outside your own head. Try to imagine how the situation would look on video, or how you would describe the setup if asked by, say, an auditor, detective, or leader in your field. Close your eyes while developing a vision of how that would play out.

Asking the right questions here helps identify the core issue as theft, and that still doesn't make figuring out how to handle the situation any easier. In some ways, it makes it harder. If the complexities of coexisting with the other valets occupy most of your attention, that frames the issue differently than when you focus on the sleight of hand involved in reusing tickets being theft, fraud, or lost income for the owner. So what do you do?

Bear in mind that committing theft makes you less trustworthy. Changing the label for your conduct as you think privately about it does not alter how others will view it if (when) it becomes known. Nor does minimizing or justifying the act by the way others behaved, or rationalizing about the special circumstances of the situation. Project yourself into a future where you're the boss and you learn that a job applicant you are seriously considering hiring has stolen money in a previous job. Would you hire such a person? Would it change how you thought about the person? Would knowing that it was only for a summer and not very much money sway your assessment of the person's suitability to work for you? What if the prospective job involved handling cash?

Sometime students addressing this scenario interject that it's hard to get a summer job, and that the job has a very short duration. These things may be true. Now, consider also who you are and what you stand for. What do you risk if you go along with a system like this? If it is a pattern in the way this operation does business, you are putting yourself at risk if an auditor catches on to what they are doing, or if there is video surveillance of the parking lot that shows the conduct. Perhaps the chances of being caught are low, but if you associate with thieves, you can become a thief—without overtly recognizing the moment as it passes you by.

Maybe there will be no tangible consequences, this time. Whether there are or not, you will know you've crossed a line. Remember that, after crossing it once, it gets easier to cross it the next time; the greatest risk could be that your choice contributes to changing you and lowering your internal bar for how you behave. If you do not identify the core issues in a situation accurately, it can be hard even to find the line when you must make a very hard choice and none of the options are appealing.

The Tennis Pro and the Airline Tickets

> You are a tennis pro at a club where an airline pilot is taking lessons. He offers you a voucher for an airplane ticket in exchange for a free lesson. You take him up on the offer, and use the voucher to go see your family. When you return, your boss, the head of the pro shop, tells you directly that you cannot give away tennis lessons, even though you know for a fact that he has done that for the airline pilot himself. What do you do, now that you have used the voucher but not held up your end of the deal?

Students discussing this scenario typically focus on the hypocrisy of the boss and question whether they want to continue to work for a liar. They also brainstorm about ways to make restitution to the pilot, either by paying for the tennis lesson out of their pockets, or by giving him his lesson on their own time at a public court.

What is less obvious about this situation and usually takes a while to emerge in the discussion is that both the pro and the pilot are trading items that are not theirs to trade. As a tennis pro, you are paid by the club to give lessons, so giving them away is costing the club income. The pilot is giving away vouchers that are intended for use by airline employees and their families, not to be sold, transferred, or bartered away. In the end, trading something that is not yours for something of personal benefit is theft—not "a clever bargain" or even "creating value." It is taking something that belongs to someone else and converting it into something for yourself.

Constructing and Rehearsing Personal Scripts

Anticipating the broad categories of difficult situations that frequently come up across a working life and preparing scripts responding to each of them is a way to compensate for lack of experience in the professional world. If you know your core values and your boundaries—What are you willing to do for money or in the service of ambition?—you will be ready to compose such scripts from a running start. If you've cataloged your strengths and your weaknesses, scripts can help you play to the former and minimize the latter. Practice identifying problems and rehearsing responses to them, and your prospects increase for preventing them from undermining your professional future. Rehearsing involves more than just thinking about these situations; you are far more likely to have words at your command, especially when you must react quickly, if you have said the words out loud a few times in private or, even better, in practice with friends. Saying them in a rehearsal, however contrived or uncomfortable it may feel, vastly increases your ability to summon the words when you most need them under pressure.

My friend and colleague Harriett Weatherford, who had a career in administration at the University of Illinois, taught me the importance of having some ready responses for when you cannot create them in the moment. She calls herself a "second-day reactor." We've all been there: someone says something to you and you don't have a quick comeback on the spot. On the second day, after you've had the chance to reflect, you have the perfect thing to say—if only you'd thought of it at the time.

Knowing herself well, and knowing about her reaction time, Harriett always liked to have what she called "key sentences" prepared and ready to go. These will vary in detail for each person, and should always include, at least, words you can use if you find yourself in a circumstance where you need time to think, or get advice, or work through your decision-making framework, or consult the rules—you get the idea.

There are two broad categories of personal scripts: *preemptive,* planned in advance either for general application (like buying time) or for use in a specific context you can anticipate, such as questioning the boss's expenses; and *reactive,* when you have to respond in real time without losing your balance. Each has its own constraints and rhythms that will affect how you prepare.

Preemptive Scripts

The components of a script for buying time to think should include both deference to the person and the importance of the request (or command) just made and some self-deprecating statement to soften or defuse a harsh reaction. The deference can be shown by how you say what you say in your script; the self-deprecation will be aided by body language and tone.

Some examples that might help you deflect requests without giving offense or appearing sanctimonious or judgmental:

Wow, I really need a little time to reflect. Will it be okay to tell you in twenty minutes?

Would it be okay with you if I write this down and get back to you tomorrow with a considered answer?

I'm so rushed right now I couldn't do justice to that. I'll carve out some dedicated time Wednesday afternoon.

Let me recheck all the numbers and get back to you in the morning.

Since I want to get things right for you, I'll circle back tomorrow to confirm my understanding and a proposed approach.

Depending on the context, it can be helpful to include your desire to protect the other person by fully complying with relevant regulations, handbooks, requirements, and so on:

I have some things I'd like to check so that you are completely covered when we file the response.

I think there is something about that in the manual they just had me sign for orientation. I'll review that to make sure I do this by the book so it doesn't reflect poorly on our group.

When you're new, ask an experienced professional you trust how he or she handles requests to buy time, or for advice on an approach that might work in your setting. In some workplaces there are touchstones or corporate foundation principles you can call upon. In other instances, simply playing dumb can be a response that will buy you a little time. If you keep asking questions that verge on the dense, sometimes the person asking you to do something that makes you uncomfortable would rather not have to be explicit and will give up. It is critical to think about how to buy some time in advance, and there will come moments when you are thankful.

Physical acts can be part of your script, too. I once coached an administrator I'll call John Cross, who had a sometimes explosive temper that was badly compromising his effectiveness. Since he knew himself fairly well, he could recognize the signals of a building outburst. What John had trouble doing, though, was stopping it before he boiled over. After a lot of trial and error, we hit upon a successful strategy. He learned to buy himself some time to calm down at those moments by knocking over his ever-present cup of coffee. He didn't need to use it very often, but when he needed it, he really needed it. The intervening moments of mop-up and apology would provide him a chance to reign himself in and avoid the explosion. This has worked well for him, and he has rocketed upward in his career. (He does have a reputation for being clumsy now, though.) It's an extreme approach to managing himself. It's still better than having people be afraid of him. It's a useful if somewhat extreme way of taking responsibility for how he affects others in his environment.

In a really awkward circumstance, precipitating a minor "accident" like John's can buy some time and space. That was just what I once needed when, in a very public place, someone who had been doing everything in her power to undermine me professionally—and not subtly—advanced on me with her arms open, as if to hug me. To avoid the encounter and to avoid saying something I knew I'd regret, I dropped my jammed-full shoulder bag on the highly polished lobby floor, scattering pens, folders, papers, and coins far and wide. The resulting chaos bought me time and distance. While I was embarrassed about being a klutz in a public place, I avoided a worse scene, and the people with me understood what was going on.

Scripts Planned for Anticipated Events

Assuming you're not instantly on the spot—or that you have managed to buy yourself some breathing room to think about things—work through the decision-making framework methodically to ensure that you understand the situation as well and fully as you can in preparation for constructing your script.

Think of a similar situation where you already know what you ought to do, so what you are seeking is the right way to do it. Even then, stop for a moment to be sure that your diagnosis of the situation is not affected by any of the cognitive errors or rationalizations that can bias your professional judgment. If you're sure, you're ready to construct your script.

The goal of your preparation is to help you modulate the tone of the interaction. Your overriding aim should be to keep the participants open to the discussion instead of shutting down. If you are initiating the conversation and have the option of choosing the time, bear in mind that just because you are ready does not mean those with whom you need to speak are. This warning applies across the board: if you are preparing to talk with a colleague or someone over whom you have power, and is especially important when that other person is a boss.

As part of your preparation, assess your role in this interaction. The opening should flow from whatever that is. If you are higher on the power curve than the other participant, convey through your opening that you are seeking a real exchange (if you are), not a charade in which judgments have already been made. (If your mind is closed, don't bother staging a conversation. Just deliver the bad news with as much compassion for others as possible, letting them preserve as much dignity as you can.)

Aim for a problem-solving conversation that might include saying hard things, without having a confrontation. Steering clear of high emotion or aggression is key. "That's the stupidest thing I've ever heard" won't elicit, "I see your point, thank you." Persuasion doesn't work by insulting, contradicting, or shouting down the other person. One of the most helpful mantras from the negotiation literature is this: try to be hard on the problem and soft on the people.

*Difficult Situation in the Face
of Possible Wrongdoing*

Not long ago, a student turned in a paper in my class on professional responsibility that contained statements that did not seem to be true. The student was writing about attending a required event, yet the attendance records did not show the student's presence. It is easy to react with anger or to rush into a condemnation. It is also easy to take it personally when someone provides information you think cannot be true. How could you think I'm so stupid? How could you do this to me? However it feels, though, this is not about you—it's about the other person.

The matter was serious, so before speaking with the student, I needed a script. (He needed a script, too.) We already had the assignment, the attendance records, and the paper he turned in. My goal was to elicit all the information, set the tone for the interaction, and stick to my role in the situation. The issues included that not only did I have responsibilities to that individual student, it was also my job to provide a level playing field for all the students in the class: Credit for work that followed the rules should not be diluted by a shortcut by a student who did not. Being fair to everyone required facts. Before going too far, I sought advice confidentially from another experienced teacher to double check that I hadn't missed important signals, jumped to unsupportable conclusions, or otherwise misread the situation.

In constructing a script, I wanted to consider alternative possibilities and not jump to conclusions. Was it possible the student had been present at the event, perhaps late, in the balcony, or somehow not seen by the others present? Had he misunderstand something about the assignment? Finally, to be fully prepared, I consulted the Student Code of Conduct, which covered the range of options available if the student's responses did not assuage my concerns.

Considering both my duty to provide fairness to the other students and possible alternative explanations led directly to a set of questions to pose at the beginning of the conversation. My aim was a neutral opening setting out the parameters and process and listing my responsibilities to all the students in the course. I began along these lines:

> I am confused by an apparent conflict between your paper and the attendance records. My duty is to apply the same requirements to all students.

Then, to make an opening for him, I structured the conversation:

> I hope you will be willing to share your reactions with me. Can you help me understand the conflict?

In any conversation that requires a script (and many that do not) it's essential to concentrate on the other person and what he or she is saying. Using the "Can you help me understand?" opening conveys an interest in hearing the other person's perspective, does not prejudge the situation, and is an open-ended question inviting response. It also provides a face-saving out if your initial concerns or conclusions were wrong. And it's much more likely to elicit a constructive answer than an accusation.

My script included the possible penalties in the Student Code of Conduct, clearly setting out the consequences, ranging from a zero on the assignment to seeking expulsion. The student turned red, coughed, and admitted he had not attended the event. I had prepared a script in case the situation was a misunderstanding ("I'm so relieved to learn this. Let me verify what you've said and then we'll consider the matter closed.") and one for this eventuality. I expressed my disappointment and sadness, summarized what the student had told me, and then ended with my closing:

> You will submit an explanation of how this happened in a class on professional responsibility by Friday at 5. After that, I will get back to you by e-mail with my decision.

The student submitted his explanation, including an apology for his "misjudgment." It didn't much help, as it was hard to get around the fact that, in an ethics class, he'd told a premeditated lie (in writing) because he wanted to avoid a late penalty and was too embarrassed to ask for an extension due to his poor planning. I failed him on the assignment, which lowered his course grade significantly, and reported the matter to the dean's office so it would be included in the student's file in the event another incident occurred. Facing the embarrassment of his bad time management, as awful as it might have felt in the moment, and taking the (lesser) consequence for that would have been a better trade-off.

Revisiting Signing When the Boss Says

Think back to the awkward situation where your boss wants you to sign off on his travel vouchers (Chapter 3). Try to isolate the root issue. The least serious possibility is that the boss is seeking reimbursement for expenses that he actually incurred, and he was just careless about keeping receipts. That would be ignoring the rule in your organization that every reimbursement requires documentation, not padding his expense account. Perhaps you have serious questions about whether the expenses were legitimate or even that they were incurred.

The regulations require that you certify that you have seen and verified the original receipts, and that you must sign your name for the process to go forward. No matter what your personal belief, and even though you wouldn't personally benefit from approving the reimbursement without the requisite receipts, you would be party to an improper transaction if you signed your name to the voucher. You would be the one (or one of the ones) on the line if that reimbursement were to be audited and you were asked to produce the receipts, which should be in your file. Meanwhile your boss is pressuring you (via his assistant) to get him his reimbursement. You know working life is a lot better and the prospects for promotion are more promising if your direct supervisor is happy with you.

If you have from the start established a reputation as a straight arrow, your path is easier than it would be if you are known for taking a shortcut here and there—especially if the boss has seen you take those shortcuts. If you are known for caring about a by-the-book approach, no one will be very surprised if you call or send a note to the assistant and say, "I'll be happy to process all the receipts I have in hand, and I'll process the remainder of the reimbursement as soon as I get the rest of the receipts. If it would help, I can provide the forms the boss can file certifying that he lost them, and I can set him up with the person who can provide an exception." If necessary, you can add the softening phrases that include how this will protect him. This is what my friend did in the real-life situation on which this is based; the boss tried to process it on his own and got called on it by higher-ups in the system. He withdrew the undocumented requests.

Being prepared can help you resist.

Since problems with reimbursements and expenses come up so often, here's another example.

Dinner and Dancing

Suppose you are in charge of signing off on expense accounts and your boss hands you a receipt one morning for a client dinner from the night before. He tells you he'd like you to expedite the reimbursement and hopes you can get it done today. Later that afternoon while you are working on the paperwork, you overhear his wife talking with the front desk receptionist about how much fun she had out dancing last night with her husband. Even though your boss will have to sign the paperwork, you will too, and your name will be on the line. In your training, you were told to authorize only charges that were itemized and verified. You feel caught between a rock and a hard place, because you are quite sure that it is not a great career move to question your boss's honesty.

When your boss asks you to process the reimbursement, before you act, consider. There are several possible scenarios. First, it could be that your boss took his wife and client to dinner together; second, your boss could have taken the client to dinner and later taken his wife dancing; third, he did not take the client out, and only took his wife instead. Any of these could be true. Your professional task, before you sign anything, is first to recognize that this could be a small act, either way, that could lead to trouble later. If you process a false voucher, you could be in trouble. If the transaction is legitimate and you antagonize your boss by handling it poorly, you could be in trouble. Ask questions and gather relevant additional information so you have all the facts before drawing conclusions.

Donning a professional persona will help. Visualize the most professional person you know, or even someone you've seen on television, someone who is calm, cool, collected, and nonaggressive. If you frame your next steps within your professional duties and obligations, with the most professional persona you can summon up, it will help you through this sticky situation.

Your professional persona will be factual, not accusatory. Getting information might sound like this: "I want to be sure that I do the very best job for you, so your reimbursement will come through promptly and leave you and our department protected at the next audit. The partner said in my orientation session that we are required to verify expenses and have documentation matching the approved list before processing them. Can you tell me where I can get that documentation so I can get this paid quickly as you asked?"

In this particular situation, there was a benign answer. The receipts existed and all was well. Imagine the bullets that were dodged, though, if that had not been the case. In a similar case, a student was being tested to see if she would follow the rules even in an ambiguous and difficult situation. Only after she asked for the proper documentation did anyone tell her she had just passed an important test in her probation.

Reactive Scripts

When I was in law school, I took a negotiation class. I thought I was an experienced professional, having been out in the working world for several years. In my first negotiation exercise with a partner, the opposing team asked a question we had not anticipated. An honest answer would have lost us the exercise, and we had no good response prepared. On his notepad beneath the table, my partner wrote, "LIE!" I was uncomfortable telling a bald-faced lie, and yet it did seem like the only way out. Rather feebly, I asked if we could have a break—giving away that we were in a weak position. My partner was furious with me, and we lost ground. I hadn't prepared for the hard questions that were likely to come up, and I didn't have a script for buying time.

When I was teaching a legal negotiation class many years later, I asked local lawyers to perform negotiation exercises for my students. I saw one of the best examples I've ever seen of a professional managing a situation like the one I flubbed so badly in law school. A participating lawyer faced with a question he hadn't anticipated, simply responded in his normal, pleasant tone, "Now, that's not a question I'm going to answer. You know that." The opposing lawyer simply moved on, never thinking a thing about what had just happened.

The response can be easy—if you can come up with words you can think up and say with ease in the moment when you need them. By envisioning and practicing in advance a wide range of situations likely to go with your professional territory, you can have a broad repertoire.

Revisiting the Intern Assigned to Pose as a Customer

Think back to the intern who posed as a customer to gather competitive information and the hard choice that confronted her. She chose to make the calls, despite her misgivings, and it cost her dearly. What could she have done instead? First, remember the preparation that would have served her in the crunch. If she had explored her values, knew the ethical standards of the industry, and recognized the danger signals in the situation before it arose, she would have been ahead of the game. If she had a personal script describing her values, she could have used it to respond. A script in a situation like this could be, "I am happy to explore another way to get this information, because I would be so uncomfortable posing as someone I'm not that I could not do a good job for you."

If she had said something like this quietly and without anger or heat, simply as a statement, with reinforcement about the willingness to do research to find the information in other ways, it would have been disarming, or at least would have bought her a little time. In a situation that catches you off guard, when you are not self-possessed enough to respond quickly and in the moment with a clear statement of your values, falling back on the structured decision-making approach might help buy some time, especially if you focus on the boss's goal—getting information—and offer to seek other ways to get there.

Using the "ask questions" approach can also work. If the questions are framed as your way of thinking through or doing a good job on the assigned task, it is hard to malign your good intent. It is always possible that you'll be accused of being slow on the uptake, but better new and ignorant than malleable and relaxed about the truth. Ask for suggestions about what to say in the calls and how to answer questions. If those you are asking want to know more about why you are calling, after all, you will need to have good answers to be plausible. If the boss is impatient with your questions, ask if you could speak with someone else about the details of the assignment, or if the boss could put the assignment in writing. Or ask if you could have some time to think about it, or to research best practices for gathering competitive intelligence according to the industry's advocacy group. Most industries have such groups and have stated standards. The intern in the real case wasn't plausible when calling competitors and did get caught in the act because of it.

Guidelines for Constructing Scripts

Gretchen Winter, my partner in designing the course Business 101: An Introduction to Professional Responsibility, and I developed the following guidelines for constructing scripts.

Set the Tone with a Neutral Opening, Using Low-Key Language

> Is this a good time to talk? I'd like to understand . . .

> Can we discuss the report?

> At the training session, the handouts we received provided a different interpretation. Do they not apply in this situation?

> I'd like to understand more about why . . .

> I might have misunderstood. Could you explain the policy to me again?

Soften your introductory phrases to leave room for resolving a misunderstanding. Strip all judgmental, accusatory, blaming, or angry words out of anything you say. Avoid adjectives. A mark of professional conduct is exhibiting restraint and understatement in pursuing information and redress when you see a problem, disagree with a course of action, or believe you have been slighted. (As a revered colleague of mine says, "Contrary to popular belief, being disagreeable is not evidence of having high standards.")

Use a Sincere Compliment plus Request

> You have taught me so much already; I'm hoping you'll have time to talk me through a question I have. I am having trouble reconciling what seems like two contradictory instructions. Can you help me understand where I'm going wrong?

> I admire the way you handle tough situations, and I am hoping that you might give me some advice on a problem I'm facing.

The same compliment-plus-request formula should also be used when asking advice about your problem if you're seeking it from someone with more power in the workplace than you have. But as with all compliments, find something true to say or don't say it. Human beings have strong hypocrisy detectors, and an insincere statement will work against the goals of your script. If you do not admire the way the person you are addressing handles tough situations, then find something else nice to say, preferably something that keys into the kind of problem you're trying to solve:

> You've repeatedly led constructive hard discussions in meetings I've attended, and I wonder if you could help me figure out if that's what I should be doing now.

> Your job requires so many tough calls, you surely have seen problems like this before. Can you help me understand . . . ?

Stay Factual; No Editorializing, Feelings,
or Attribution of Motives
This is the place to censor every single thing you say, and your thoughts if you can. Make no assumptions and avoid sharing emotions. Stick to evidence and whatever facts you have. Leave options open for the chance that you've misunderstood or overlooked an important element.

Use "I" Not "You"

> I'm confused . . . ; I'm concerned about . . . ; I wonder . . .

Ask Questions

> Why do we do it this way?

> Who else does it this way?

> How will this affect . . . ?

> Have I understood properly?

> Is there someone who could help me understand?

> Did I receive a copy of that? My records do not show receipt.

Leave Time and Conversational Openings for the Other to Respond (and Then Listen)

I'd like to explain my concerns and then I hope you will be willing to share your reactions with me.

Focus on what's being said and strive to understand it from the other perspective.

Thank the Other Person

This step is important; like giving credit, it wins goodwill. In a positive tone of voice, thank the other person for listening, for reflecting on the situation with you, for making recommendations, and for taking time to help you find an answer to your question.

Agree on a Time, Place, and Method for Follow-Up (If Desirable or Required)

I appreciate your help today. I'm making a note to call you again on Thursday the 30th to check on the paperwork.

You will submit an explanation of how this happened by Friday at 5. After that, I will get back to you by e-mail with my decision about how to respond to this matter.

Thank the other person again.

Revisiting the Campus Bookstore Employee Discount

In your bookstore job, you face pressure from your budget and pressure from your friends to use your employee discount. There are plenty of ways to rationalize what you might be tempted to do, since it will solve so many serious problems for you. Ask yourself what you are willing to do for money, and why.

If you look at this closely, while you could figure you are just being clever, it is at base stealing because it deprives the bookstore of its profit margin. If you are discovered, you will probably lose your job and you could be prosecuted. Imagine asking your manager if you can use your employee discount to subsidize your income and sell books, with a markup, to your friends. If, given the environment in the bookstore, you can imagine doing that and having it go well, ask away. If the boss both appears to have the authority to give permission (and is not himself just colluding with you to cheat the system) and gives you that permission, ask for it in writing, and then sally forth on this scheme. Why get permission in writing? To protect yourself later if the permission was not legitimate and to show that you took reasonable precautions so that, in the worst-case scenario where this is part of a sting operation or a later investigation (both real outcomes of situations I have seen—remember all those misconduct cases?), you are not swept up with the bad guys.

Pose this question as you ponder your course of action: What if everyone did it? If everyone did this, the bookstore might stop offering any employee discounts, or, in the worst case, go out of business. That still may not make it any easier to come up with what to say to your friends when you turn them down. If those words come easily to you, skip ahead. For many, the biggest dilemma in this situation is how to say no without sounding too sanctimonious and without losing friends.

While it might be tempting to try to expand one of the personal perquisites of your job into more money, the real problem here is that, even with the job and the discount, you are still coming up short in your budget. Options to address that real problem include asking for a promotion or a raise, looking for a better job, trying to figure out other ways to save money so you have more for a social life (maybe your friends have space for a roommate and you could all save money on rent), or talking to your college about whether you might be eligible for other financial aid, and so on. Once you define the real problem and ask the right questions, you can come up with solutions other than cheating on your personal discount— and putting your job and your reputation on the line.

If you managed a delay in responding to your friends while you reflected on your response, and you have thought about your values and have a way to articulate them, you will have an easier task responding than if you have not. Prepare for a full set of options, starting with the truth: "I could get fired, and I really need this job."

If the person dares you or suggests you are just afraid, you have two options. One is to stick with the truth and say, "You are right. I am, because I really need this job." Agreeing often takes the wind out of the sails of aggression. Or you could agree and also add a statement of your values to underline your position: "Yeah, no matter how tempting it is to make myself some money and save you some, too, that is just not something I think I could do and [choose here: get away with, or, live with myself afterward]." It's pretty hard to disagree with a defining statement of someone's values, stated sincerely and quietly, and without challenge to anyone else's choices.

Another approach would be to defer to authority and suggest you could try asking your boss: "I'll ask the boss if I can use my discount that way, and if she says yes, we're on." Or if you are genuinely surprised that your friend thought you might do that, you could say, "I'm really sorry if anything I've done gives the impression that I would cheat my boss." Alternatively, if the situation permits, make a joke of the whole thing: "Sure, and after that, let's rob the bank next door and we'll split the loot."

Each of these approaches articulates your values and puts money in its proper place in your life, which is subordinate to your sense of self and your values.

Having scripts you have created in your own words for predictable situations, which you have practiced so they are in your mental muscle memory, will smooth your responses in heading off problems.

Another tool that you can start practicing now to good benefit is one that can improve your self-expression—the And Stance.

The And Stance

William Ury and his colleagues at Harvard's Project on Negotiation were pioneers in introducing a powerful technique for creating constructive, problem-solving interactions they dubbed the And Stance. The essence of this skill, expanded on in Ury's book *Getting Past No*,

An article published earlier this summer in a prestigious journal scooped us, reporting on eighteen samples, while we've looked at over a thousand and haven't seen even once what they claim to see. We cannot get our data published because "the literature" (i.e., their paper) contradicts our findings. Another paper this group published in that same prestigious journal included images which, on close examination using one of the methods we learned in an ethics class to detect fraudulent data, are composites of three different images. It's clear that the images have been tampered with.

So, we think this group has a history of publishing unacceptably manipulated, and perhaps even fraudulent, data. We want to address both the fact that our data are much stronger than theirs, and that they have history of submitting misleading data to this journal. Should we be doing anything beyond that? Should we be reporting this to the funding agency's misconduct office?

First, let's figure out what the issues are.

- Jordan's group cannot get their data published because of the existing suspect paper.
- They believe the paper contains fabricated data.
- The scooping group has a prestigious publishing track record (Jordan's does not).
- Jordan wants justice.
- But not at the expense of delaying her own research and publishing.
- It's important not to show too much of her data in a complaint, as that could preempt later publication.

Thinking this through systematically shows a potential pitfall: even though the results of a thousand samples are far more meaningful than the report based on a mere eighteen, it is critical to preserve Jordan's ability to publish later, elsewhere if necessary.

What are the rules and regulations? These are not complicated to identify: telling the truth, the need for accuracy in the literature, and university and federal regulations about research integrity and misconduct.

What questions must you ask and answer here in order to decide how to proceed?

- What might legitimately explain the published results?
- What are the possible reasons for the image anomalies?
- How might this situation look from the editor's perspective?
- What are the possible reactions to a letter from Jordan's group?

Some basic realities of the publishing world will restrict the editor's options:

- He doesn't have the primary data, didn't do the work, and probably isn't a specialist on the particular, narrow topic of the paper.
- His job is to judge the manuscript and the peer reviews, not the work itself.
- He might not have the training himself or access to a specialist who can determine if the images were fabricated.

Examining the editor's options reveals that he could take few actions other than to refer the whole matter to the paper's authors. Jordan and her colleagues must think through the consequences of a limited range of options on the other end.

There's more to the problem than that, though. As Jordan thinks through a possible course of action, she should imagine that the authors might be friends, or at least powerful colleagues, of the editor. One thing she might do, then, is to address the letter to more than one person, so ideally there would have to be a conversation between them before simply referring it to the authors. In any event, she will need to focus on her common ground with the editor, which is wanting the data published in his journal to be accurate and reputable.

Given the seriousness of the professional questions facing her, Jordan must strive to achieve a tone that is as impersonal and non-accusatory as possible. It's the data that are at odds here, not the people. She must not appear to accuse anyone of anything. At the same time, her objective is to make the issues surrounding the data and images as clear as possible so the editor cannot miss them. Put yourself in Jordan's shoes, and imagine being at the bottom of the power curve, trying to get questions addressed about work by far more powerful people in your field.

The resources in the situation are the rules of the game and the editor's interest in accurate publications in his journal. This leaves Jordan to construct a course of action that preserves her reputation and professional choices, no matter how this turns out. Here are the possible actions she developed:

- Writing the most polite, dispassionate letter possible, focusing on the conflicting data, not the personalities, and stressing what she doesn't understand.
- Publishing elsewhere (after all, the result of examining 1,000 samples should trump that of examining 18).

She chose the first option. Here's the beginning of the letter she wrote the editor, trying to adopt a professional tone and posing issues to be addressed without giving her own data away:

Dear _____,

Our group is working on X, so we have been most interested in the papers published in your journal on that topic in 2005 and 2009. The 2005 paper, with a sample size of N, and the 2009 paper, with the same N, report Y. Our own review of a greater number of samples is at variance with that result and leads instead to a finding of Z. The variance of other published data as well as our own with that in the two papers is most evident when examining the images. The topic of X is a critical one in the area, with many researchers likely seeking to understand it. We look forward to additional information that will clarify apparent conflicts in the published data.

This letter very effectively puts that "variance" in the data front and center and not only invokes (obliquely) the common ground about the accuracy of data, it also draws in the interests of the "many researchers" in the field who might have similar questions. It uses the And Stance to contrast the variance between the greater number of samples and a different finding.

The note raises the potential importance of the matter to the editor without setting up a confrontation and effectively poses the issues without applying any labels. It is probably about as strong a letter as someone in Jordan's position can send. At this writing, I do not know how this story ends. Jordan, meanwhile, is working on publishing her data elsewhere, still working to overcome the pollution in the literature from data she believes are flawed that are preventing hers from appearing. Even in the worst case, where the editor does nothing, Jordan has left herself as many options as possible and can continue to work, gathering additional data and perhaps another slant on the problem so that her data will see the light of day. In this case she must play the long game.

And what about reporting the discrepancies her team perceives to the federal funding agency? That's a harder call, since, without a response to the letter, it's hard to know whether there are facts she has not considered that might provide an explanation. Failing a response from the editor, it might be time for Jordan to seek advice from someone of stature in her field, to see if that person can help explain the situation or expresses a view as to whether the apparently constructed images should be reported.

When you're put on the spot in a situation that feels like a dilemma, whenever possible, use a pre-prepared script that you have practiced before so it comes out smoothly to buy yourself some breathing room to think things through so you can react calmly and professionally. The more the other person is being critical of you or nasty, the more important it is that you manage yourself to avoid an aggression spiral, no matter how natural it is to flame back. Keep your long-term goals and reputation in mind, and focus on the professional persona you are building—and want to maintain.

When you face a situation needing a personal script, use the decision-making framework methodically to ensure that you understand the situation as well and fully as you can.

How you handle conflict situations will as much as anything you do define your professional persona. Choose who you want to be and use the tools at your disposal to achieve your goals.

CHAPTER 5

How to Have a Dispute Professionally

Let's say you've started learning to recognize the signals, thought long and hard about your values and the lessons of misconduct, learned the rules of your organization and profession for ethical practices, considered your professional persona, practiced the And Stance, and developed some great personal scripts. Still, you find yourself facing a problem at work. It happens. Don't panic. Remember that while you don't get to change the other people in a situation, you always control what you do, and that how you approach problems will shape their outcomes.

Even more, there's a systematic procedure—a set of practical rules—you can study, review, and rely on for support when you face a conflict. These are things that experts know and novices do not. They are things you can learn. They all use the earlier habits and tools, so roll all you've learned so far into learning how to have a dispute professionally.

The Basics

The single most important thing any time you face a problem is to heed the wisdom of the old saying, "Never attribute to malice that which incompetence will explain," and the Knoll corollary, "Never attribute to incompetence that which temporary inattention or misunderstanding will explain."

Most problems start because of mistakes, oversights, and miscommunication, not bad intent or a desire to do you wrong. More critically, if you start with the operating assumption that somehow wires have gotten crossed and you set about sorting them out with a problem-solving attitude, you'll fare better even in the rarer case where there was malice at work. Plus, you'll be right most of the time. Others will observe and respect your restraint, and your approach will reflect positively on you as a professional and contribute to the reputation you are building.

Problems are best resolved at the level closest to the people involved, using actual information, not your conclusions, inferences, or surmises.

If you are in a wrangle with a colleague, it's easy to start avoiding the person because it might be uncomfortable or awkward to talk directly—especially if you know or suspect that you contributed to the problem. If you spend your time talking with other people about the situation, while it's possible that you might learn something useful, you are also likely to be increasing your own level of stress, and you could open yourself to the perception that you're just stirring the pot instead of trying to solve the problem.

Say someone lets you down by not providing an analysis you need for an important report. It can be tempting, and feel easier, just to do the work yourself (making a note that person is unreliable) to avoid a confrontation. It's not so easy to find a good script to address someone's shortcomings, after all, especially if you like is to excise the word "but" from your vocabulary and replace it in most instances with the word "and," even when you are expressing disagreement. Changing how you say things does not need to change what you mean. It just improves the likelihood that your views will be heard and considered. With Ury's permission, I constructed a set of exercises to help leaders and students I work with master the skill. Read Ury's book, use the samples in the appendix to practice, and then start using the And Stance regularly. If you can master the skill and make it a habit, it will have both preventive and defusing effects and make your work life a more constructive one.

The idea behind the And Stance is that the word "but" is a stopper word: when people hear it, they shut down, anticipate criticism, and become defensive. This happens for a reason: we frequently use "but" as a signal that criticism is coming, even when we try to soften it by saying something nice first: "That's a great shirt, but do you think orange is a good color with your skin tones?"

The And Stance is probably the hardest of the key tools to master because of how much we use "but . . ." to disagree, criticize, and generally assume oppositional postures with others without acknowledging directly that we're fighting. (The *Oxford English Dictionary*'s Corpus reports that "but" is the twenty-second most commonly used word in English.)[1] Pay attention to conversations around you and count the number of times people precede criticism with a "but," or use the word as a way to interrupt and seize control of a situation, insert distance between the speakers, or put someone else down. In most of the ways it's used in everyday conversations, "but" escalates tension; we use it to put a nice face on disagreements and shove aside the views of others.

After teaching the And Stance to thousands of people, I can predict that you might be skeptical. Try it before you reject it.

Feel the difference in the following comments that could be written on a report. First the typical way: "The first five pages are very good, but your organization and argument deteriorate after that." Now, shift your response to the And Stance:

The first five pages are very good and if the rest matched its organization and argument, it would be a very strong report.

The first five pages are very good and I'd like to work with you on ways to bring all of the report up to that standard.

The first five pages are very good and we should talk about ways to strengthen the organization and argument after that.

Compare this kind of feedback to the "but" example above. Which would you prefer to receive in response to something you've written? Which would be most likely to keep you motivated and feeling good about continuing to work on and revise your report?

Say someone working for you asks for a day off. You cannot approve the request for that day, and you say so in the usual way: "I'd like to be able to grant your request for that day off, but I know we will be short staffed that day already." It's a turn-down, and you've been a good boss by explaining your reasons. Compare these alternative versions that use the And Stance:

I'd like to be able to grant your request for a day off and if we weren't already going to be short staffed that day, I'd be able to do it.

I'd like to be able to grant your request for a day off, and if you'd asked earlier, we might have been able to work it out.

I'd like to be able to grant your request for a day off and since we're short staffed already that day, would another day that week work just as well for you?

A faculty member in a department and discipline that were badly riven with long-standing disputes about methodology told me she'd tried using the And Stance and was astonished at the results: by consistently lowering the temperature of conversations through its use, seeking information (and listening to it), and phrasing her disagreements using the And Stance, she managed to achieve a civil working relationship with her major antagonist. The two of them were able to frame a proposal for their disciplinary society that helped set boundaries for the two warring camps so they could both do their work. The camps never came to like each other—no one really changed anyone else's mind—and they were able to find a way to coexist productively without the open warfare that had characterized their meetings for far too long. Used effectively, the And Stance is a powerful tool of persuasion, influence, and conflict reduction.

Moving to the And Stance doesn't mean changing your mind or your message (the report is still not good enough; the answer for the day off is still no). What it does do is to change how you communicate so the other person is more likely to absorb what you have to convey and be more motivated to work with you cooperatively.

The And Stance can be the most powerful tool in this book, and its use is entirely under your control. No one else is even slightly involved in your decision to practice and deploy it. If you can master it, you will be amazed at its effectiveness in the face of disagreements with other people at work and about work-related topics. (Note that using the And Stance does not mean you can replace "but" with "however" or "although." They are just softer words with the same effect.)

If you are worried that this could be manipulative, remember that how you use a tool is your responsibility: All tools can be used for both positive and negative ends. After all, a hammer can be used to build a wall or to destroy it. The hammer itself is not inherently good or bad. You can use the And Stance to build bridges and increase the common ground in a situation, or otherwise. After you've learned how to use the tool, then you can decide whether it is useful to you and, if so, when and how to deploy it.

Using the And Stance has two distinct effects. First, you change your alignment with the other person by changing the way you think and express yourself. Second, using agreement and eliminating as many stopper words and barriers as possible improves the chances your audience will hear, absorb, and retain what you are trying to communicate.

A good way to practice the And Stance is through e-mail. Set yourself a goal of not using "but" in writing for a week or until you get the hang of it. After that, try to use it in conversation consistently for a week. Pay attention to how this small change affects the tone of your interactions and how you think about the situations you face. In most discussions at work, reducing the friction in solving problems is worthwhile, saving time, preserving and building relationships, and getting things done. Once you've practiced and mastered the tool, consider when and where it is most effective for you. There are always occasions when you want to punctuate your disagreements, and "but" can be effective for setting contrasts and highlighting differences.

The And Stance can help lower the emotional temperature and keep a discussion more solution focused and civil. It increases alignment, it's free, it's invisible, and it's entirely under your own control. Its use will say a lot about you, to yourself and to others. After all, how you behave in difficult situations will be one of the characteristics that distinguishes you from others and shapes your reputation. Give it a shot.

Bringing It All Together

Here's a dilemma in which the person sought advice not about how to handle her own conduct, but how to address a consequential professional lie by others. The same decision-making approach and careful alignment with others we've been exploring can help work through this complex situation, too. See if you can translate this situation to your own environment as you go through it.

Was the Scoop Faked?

A student working in a new lab sought advice on confronting the publication of possibly fraudulent data by competing researchers. Let's call the student Jordan. Jordan said:

seen as balanced and will fare better in the long term, no matter how uncomfortable that might be in the moment. Say directly, "My action might have made this worse, and if it did, I am sorry about that and I want to do what I can to make it better."

Not only will understatement help you resolve problems more effectively and quickly with those directly affected, consistently expressing yourself dispassionately and courteously will persuade those removed from the heat of the battle (think: your boss) that your perspective deserves careful consideration.

As you aim to separate the personal from the professional, remember the effects of the sinister attribution bias, which is triggered when you dislike a person. That makes it easier for you to ascribe bad motives to the person—and the favor will be returned in the face of your hostility. Aggression spirals can result, because we tend to feel the attacks of others more powerfully than they assess them to be.

Through clever experiments, Daniel Wolpert and his colleagues have shown how this effect leads to rapid escalation of hostilities. In one experiment, Wolpert devised a way to measure the force applied when one participant prodded another.[1] He asked each one to poke the other person back with the same force. In theory, the pokes should have started and stayed at the same level and never increased. That's not what happened. Instead, the recipient of a prod perceived it as stronger than its originator did. In responding, the first recipient then escalated the force to match the perceived power of the prod. You can see where that heads.

Don't just take out the emotion in dealing with the problem directly. If you find yourself overwhelmed by anger, frustration, resentment, or anxiety as you think about the problem, find dispassionate sources of advice. Here, too, separate the professional elements from the personal parts. If you are trying to sort through the correct professional actions, don't ask or expect those you're consulting about elements of professional conduct to function as your friend or therapist. If you need one of those, you need the real thing.

Do not, not ever, conduct a disagreement by e-mail. Aggression spirals are more likely to occur in e-mail than in person. E-mail is not private—remember, all e-mail can be examined by your employer and even the general public if you work at a public institution. It is not confidential, either; you have no control of where e-mail goes after you send it. It may get forwarded anywhere. (Have you seen the e-mail that went viral from the young associate quitting a law firm intemperately? Or the one misaddressed by a CEO and sent to "all employees" instead of just his mistress, as intended?) Last and far from least, e-mail, texts, and instant messages are very difficult to get rid of; they tend to stick around on servers, backups, etc. Never put anything in e-mail that is written in the heat of the moment or could come back to haunt you. If you are having a problem with someone at work, have every conversation that you can in person, following all of the rules in this book scrupulously. It is harder for problems to escalate when you can see the other person, read his or her body language signals, and hear the words and tonal patterns. In person, you can take a break if things start to spin out of control.

Especially for serious matters, the more you can do in person, the better off you will be. When you talk, if you can only remember one technique to use, make it the next one.

Remember to Ask Questions

Remember that asking questions in a controlled and cordial tone of voice is the least confrontational way to raise concerns. Especially when a problem is brewing, frame your questions on the premise that there's something you don't understand and you're seeking help to improve your own comprehension so you can be a better contributor. Use the nonthreatening "help me understand" construct: "Can you help me understand why the report was submitted without my section being included?" or "Have I misunderstood? At orientation, they specifically instructed us to record hours we worked on every project so future staffing estimates could be managed" or "Could you show me which step I missed? I cannot make this come out the same way." Do not make accusations or attribute motives to others; keep seeking information until you have assembled as many relevant facts as possible.

It's very important to listen and not just to talk in these exchanges. Whenever you ask questions, you should be engaging in a two-way conversation, not airing your views with a question glued on the end. Conflict situations create hypersensitivities to perceived criticism. If you can get in the habit of asking questions even in your interior dialogues, you won't run the risk of slipping into presentations of conclusions rather than expressions of concern.

How you ask questions matters. Working with a dysfunctional team recently, I watched as a newish member of the group challenged an existing practice. In essence, her question was "Why do you always do it that way?" The response was quick and sharp: "Until you've been here longer, you don't know enough to chime in." (Message sent and received: "So shut up.") When I rephrased the newcomer's question to focus on the central issue using neutral vocabulary, with a gentle tone of voice and first acknowledging the expertise and time investment of the more established team member—giving him room to consider the question without feeling challenged—he recognized and acknowledged that he hadn't understood what she was asking and that the question was actually a good one. Everyone else concurred. Few had even heard the question as a question; most heard only what they took to be criticism. Too many well-meaning exchanges get derailed by similar dynamics, whether from unintended brashness by the new or from overreactive insecurity by the more established. Building the ability and skill to control your tone can avert these effects.

If your conflict is more than a misunderstanding or a personal dispute, if it concerns a central matter affecting your values or your professional obligations, you may need to go further than the basics take you. That's when you need the rules.

The Rules for Taking a Stand on Ethical Grounds

If you find yourself in that bad situation where your boss asks—or tells—you to do something that violates your sense of right and wrong, what do you do? Or maybe you see something happening that just doesn't feel right or, worse, really looks like a serious violation. You might try to raise questions and have them shut down. Then what? How do you decide whether to do anything? If you do, what it should be? If you have used all the tools so far for resolving professional disputes and they haven't worked, or if the situation is so serious you do not want to take it on informally, once again, help is available. Follow these rules while you assess what's bothering you. As you do, bear in mind the competing pressures of such situations.

The Pressure to Stay Quiet

Let's start with messages to do nothing. The pressures in group settings—work or school, for example—combine to tamp down our instinct to speak against possible wrongdoing. We tend to follow the lead of others, to conform to the group, or to rationalize that, if something is truly wrong, someone else will take care of it.

The Bystander Effect

We know that the greater the number of people who are aware of a problem, the less likely it is that any one person will step forward. It's called the bystander effect, and some of the most replicated research in social psychology has demonstrated its power across a wide range of settings. This research was catalyzed in the 1960s by news reports of a woman named Kitty Genovese who called out for help while being stabbed and raped in New York City within earshot of many people in their apartments. Trying to understand how that could have happened, Darley and Latane staged emergencies in and around groups of people.[2] From smoke pouring into a classroom to fake heart attacks, they found that the larger the number of people nearby, the less likely anyone was to respond. At the same time, they found that if one person did step forward to help, that often stimulated others to do the same.

You can be that person.

Conformity and Peer Pressure

Remember from Chapter 3 that the impulse to go along with the group, to do what everyone else is doing, can be stronger than we acknowledge or expect. Even when we think of ourselves as independent voices, willing to swim against the current, it can be surprisingly hard to withstand the pressure around us, particularly when it builds slowly and we generally like and respect the people we work with. This effect is amplified when some of those people have more power than we do, especially over our careers. Query yourself now and again, considering how much the conduct of others is affecting you. Try to think about how the situation would look to others (say, a reporter, if you had to explain it, or someone you like and admire) and how your explanations would sound. If "feeble" comes to mind as a descriptor, that's a signal.

Ambivalence about Whistle-Blowing

While in theory we believe that wrongdoing should be reported, our feelings about the practice are more ambivalent, which also adds to the pressure to follow the lead of others around us. We've all heard about what can happen to people who report what turns out to be serious wrongdoing: Sherron Watkins, the accountant at Enron who first reported the financial manipulations that eventually brought the whole company down, was the subject of an internal investigation seeking to fire her and was vilified by the company's lawyers when she testified at trial. Jeff Wigand, the scientist who reported that his tobacco company was manipulating nicotine levels in cigarettes, lost his job and his family.

In business, in government, in science: we hear all too often that people who report wrongdoing get fired for their efforts. After years of limbo, an investigation or a lawsuit may finally substantiate the original report, but the person making the report might have endured serious consequences: unemployment, reputational damage, medical or psychological problems, divorce, financial distress, and so on. We hear these stories, and they resonate with us on many levels, reinforcing messages we learned as children.

As a society, we don't much like tattletales. We don't like them as children, and we don't like them as adults. Among many reasons for this, a big one is mistrust of the motives. Is that person telling to gain advantage over others in the group? Did you tell Mom that Ben got an extra cookie so you could too, or so he would get in trouble? Or did you go to Mom and tell her what Ben was doing because the fire he set got out of control and it scared you? Those are very different situations, and their analogs recur all the time in working life. At the same time, as we get older, the stakes get higher: if you see or are part of an unethical practice or a violation of professional guidelines, not only could many others get hurt, you and your career could, too.

So Why Report?

Before you throw up your hands and decide to keep your head down and never say a word to anyone about anything going on around you, stop and consider the bigger picture. When one person, or a group, breaks the rules to benefit themselves, there are often huge costs to others. When the safety practices for deep water oil drilling were "finessed" past sensible limits on the *Deepwater Horizon,* the livelihoods and homes of hundreds of thousands of people were affected. When two scientists reported they had achieved desktop cold fusion, the time and money of scores of researchers were diverted—wasted—while trying to replicate and then investigate the false claims.

More personally, who are you and what do you stand for? Do you want your reputation associated with an organization that countenances misconduct? If your boss manipulates the sales figures for the quarter, not only could she get caught and end up without a job, you could too. If your advisor fudges data, not only could his career end, yours could be put under a lifelong cloud as well.

How do you figure out if speaking up is worth it? Should any sensible person ever blow the whistle when confronted with evidence of serious wrongdoing?

It depends.

As is so often the case, there are unwritten rules that affect how your situation will play out. Knowing and following the rules will make all the difference in what you should do and the outcome of your efforts. It is also important to know that for every story that makes the newspapers, many never become public, because the person concerned about wrongdoing followed the rules and quietly got the problem corrected. That's not news and it doesn't carry huge penalties. Speaking out against wrongdoing does show you to be a person of integrity, character, and maturity who handles problems professionally and well.

The rules kick in well before you go to file charges. They start with how you handle your concerns from the beginning and how you conduct yourself when you have disagreements with people at work about matters of import, especially ones with ethical dimensions.

Rule 1: Consider Alternative Explanations

All the following rules are based upon your total and complete compliance with this one.

It's very easy to be wrong, especially when you're just starting out, because you might not have sufficient access to all the information nor yet have a strong network to warn you when you've misread a situation. Guard against attributing motives to anyone else, and remember: it's not all about you. When someone does something, you might not have been (and probably were not) a factor in that person's thinking.

At every turn, consider seriously the fact that your perception of the situation may be mistaken. Remain open to information that provides an explanation different from your own. When receiving information that challenges your existing conclusions, go back and reexamine your logic to see if it still holds up. Rule 1 does not mandate that you ignore clear conclusions from obvious facts. It simply requires you to make a serious and considered effort to ensure that your conclusions are sound and will withstand close scrutiny by people more removed from the immediate situation. It is far better for you to perform these checks than for others to expose major flaws in your thinking that you could have discovered had you applied a sufficiently stringent standard.

When I was the person responsible for investigating academic misconduct on my campus, a student I'll call Paul came to see me about a problem he had with his advisor, whom I knew by reputation. I'll call him Professor Very Important. Paul showed me a letter Professor Important had received, inviting him to contribute a chapter to a forthcoming book. Scrawled across the letter, in what Paul said was the professor's handwriting, was a quick note: "Paul, why don't you take a stab at this?" Paul did, through eight or nine drafts. He had each version of his work with him, and I could see the progression through the extensive editing and notes on each draft, each again in the professor's handwriting. The first few efforts were so heavily marked up in red ink they looked like they'd drip on me if I wasn't careful. The final draft had another handwritten note across the top saying, "This is fine. Thanks—V. I."

Paul then told me his girlfriend did office work for his professor and had told Paul that she had put together a letter of transmission and mailed the manuscript to the editor of the volume—but only with Professor Important's name. Paul was not included as a coauthor. "Oh," I said. "That could be a problem. What did you do?"

After worrying about it overnight, Paul said, he had called his mom for advice. She counseled him to forget it, finish his degree, and get out of there. After agonizing, Paul decided he couldn't do that, however sensible it might be. He made an appointment with

Professor Important to ask about coauthorship on the chapter. The meeting hadn't gone very well. The professor confirmed the manuscript had been submitted only under his name and said, "This was a learning exercise, Paul. You'll get to coauthor things later."

He just couldn't let it pass, he said. He'd never be able to live with himself if he let this injustice stand.

Paul's situation called for a formal review of the manuscript, because this was an allegation of plagiarism. In academic life, where credit for ideas and publications controls who advances and how fast, representing the words or ideas of another as your own is a serious violation. To assure that we had all the facts, we contacted the editor to get a copy of the submitted manuscript and compared it to Paul's stack of drafts.

The chapter submitted by Professor Important bore no relationship to Paul's drafts.

Professor Important, when interviewed, told us Paul's work was so bad that it was unsalvageable. He had thrown it out and started from scratch, and the final version didn't include any of Paul's inadequate research or writing. There was no plagiarism in this situation. (Professor Important's failure to mentor his student according to university guidelines carried a serious penalty of its own, however. It's fine to judge a student's work as not up to standard, and when that happens, professors are expected to help the student learn from the experience.)

The point of this story is that Paul had taken every proper step, in keeping with the rules that follow for handling disputes, when he thought Professor Important had stolen his words: he had thought about it, he had gotten advice, he had taken his concerns directly to the person. However, given how Professor Important had (mis) handled the situation, Paul didn't have all the relevant facts, nor could he have had them. Every fact he did have suggested something unacceptable had happened. And he was still wrong.

There may be information you do not have or cannot get. You are not expected to be omniscient, but you are required to be careful and judicious in forming your opinions. No matter how firm your

conclusions, it is essential that you follow the next rule in formulating your concerns. If you can get in the habit of following it even in
your interior dialogues, you won't run the risk later of slipping into
presentations of conclusions rather than expressions of concern.

*Rule 2: Ask Questions; Do Not
Make Charges*

Good career survival skills require you at every turn to remain open
to information that provides an alternative explanation to your own.
When that information challenges your existing conclusions, consider seriously that your perception of the situation may be mistaken,
go back and reexamine your logic. Then start asking questions.

The word "questions" is critical. Before charging anyone with
anything, it is good practice to pose your concerns as questions,
particularly allowing for the fact that you might have misunderstood or misinterpreted the situation. This is especially true for employees new to a department or organization, and those low on the
power scale, who do not always have all the information necessary
for evaluating a situation.

For example, if your boss tells you to adjust the sales numbers
for the quarter in a way you think crosses the line, stop and assess
whether other sales are being reported to your boss that you don't
know about. Are divisions included in your numbers that you
don't see? Look at the organization chart and think about what
you don't know. Does the person who told you to leave out some
of the data to smooth the curve have experience with the kind
of work you're doing? What's the chance that she or someone else has
been doing additional experiments you do not know about that are
informing how she instructs you to report? In either case, there are
legitimate, nonconfrontational questions you can—and should—ask.

Frame your questions to convey the sense that you might have
missed something: "Have I misunderstood? At the training course
[orientation, college, etc.], they instructed us to record sales differently. Can you help me learn what's different about this situation so

I can do a better job next time?" "Am I misinterpreting these results? No matter how often I recalculate, I'm having trouble getting the result shown on this table in the manuscript. Can you help me see where I'm going wrong?" Steps 1 and 2 under Procedures for Responsible Whistle-Blowing also contain some relevant pointers.

*Rule 3: Figure Out What Documentation
Supports Your Concerns and Where It Is*

Playing "he said, she said" is not fun. The more you can keep the focus on factual matters, the better off you will be. You can help keep all eyes on the issues, not on your personality, by concentrating on marshaling information, as well as by presenting yourself as professionally and unemotionally as possible. If you know what the right questions are (and where the answers are, even if you don't have access to the source), you can pose them authoritatively enough that they cannot be shrugged off without examination. What numbers or procedures are at issue and why? Who collected the data and how, where can they be found, and in what form (paper, computer file, notebooks, sales reports, etc.)? Who might have useful information, and how can that person or persons be reached? What written rules or regulations apply?

All of this can be complicated when you have serious reservations about the conduct of someone with much greater power and influence than you.

A department head and a faculty member collaborated on a research project that resulted in a patent for use of a drug in a particular disease application. The department head started a company that licensed the intellectual property to develop technology based on it. The company couldn't replicate the animal data. When it looked like the company would go under, the department head started asking the faculty member about other uses for the drug based on his research. The faculty member declined to discuss his research with the department head because of the financial conflict of interest. When the faculty member went out of town for a week to attend a conference, the department head started asking the faculty member's students about their research using the drug. The students, not knowing about the conflict of interest (or the existence of the company), were happy to discuss their work with the department head.

Not only did the department head in this situation have a conflict of interest, he used his university-based power and position for his personal interests by seeking information for personal gain and his company's benefit. The conflict of interest contaminated all that followed and was the fulcrum of the dispute.

When you perceive conflict of interest in a superior, say, tread softly. Use a very structured, formal analysis of the problem. A good starting place might be a copy of the organization's policy and procedures. Given your relative positions, the more information you have about the guiding principles and structures for enforcing them, the more likely you are to be able to devise an approach to answers about the perceived conflict without jeopardizing your own position. Browse the website if there is one, or check out whatever written materials come out of the office that issues the policy and is responsible for its implementation. Think about what that policy says about the organization's mission and its suggestions for seeking balance between internal and external connections. Pay special attention to information about the responsible officers. Is there a resource for individuals to ask questions? Is there an oversight committee? Early on, learn the name of the person whose job it is to guide ethics conflicts and inquiries in keeping with the organization's policies. (And, by the way, be sure to review the terms of access for ethics hotlines should you decide to avail yourself of them: do they promise to maintain confidentiality, or not?)

Rule 4: Separate Your Personal and
Professional Concerns

It's time to apply the element of the basic habits that requires you to be completely careful that you have separated your personal and professional concerns. Present yourself only in a professional light. The importance of adhering to this rule increases with the seriousness of the situation.

Do not let the problem become one about you, your conduct, or the way you handle yourself.

Rule 5: Assess Your Goals

What are you seeking in this situation? What would it take to make you feel that it has been properly resolved? How will you know when you have achieved it? Know the answers to these questions before going any further, because they will affect your next actions.

Are you trying to get the sales numbers fixed? Get the work redone? Catalyze a public or private discussion of the issues? Correct a report to an oversight agency? Make the marketing claims more accurate? Get someone else to admit error and that you are right? Get money for supporting your own theory? Protect yourself from association with misconduct?

Long before you start asking for advice, going public, or lodging formal charges, it is critical to know what you personally seek from the situation and how you will know when you get it. These situations can escalate very quickly. Lodging charges, in particular, almost always results in a loss of control. Analyzing your own motives and goals can be very helpful in choosing the path to follow.

For example, Step 1 of the whistle-blowing procedures (below) may well lead the person you consult to become concerned as well. If control and personal involvement (as in receiving an apology or public vindication for your contribution) are important enough to you that you will be dissatisfied without personal involvement in a correction to the record, you need to know that and to articulate it in your interactions.

If you do not know what you seek before you get into this process, you may well find yourself unhappy with the outcome, no matter what it is. In addition, if you do file charges, you will almost certainly be asked what recourse you seek. Having a coherent and reasoned answer to this question will have a constructive effect on the process and will reinforce the other steps you have taken to make this a matter of professional conduct, not emotional reaction.

Rule 6: Seek Advice and Listen to It

If you have complied to the best of your ability with all these rules and still believe there is a problem, you are ready to approach the step-by-step process of responsible whistle-blowing. Note that there are still steps to go through before filing charges. You can only go so far by yourself, so this is the place where you must stop and explore your concerns with someone else.

Yes, again.

Steps 1 and 2 below provide information on picking the right person and the overriding importance of listening to the advice you receive. No matter how honest you have been with yourself or how critically you have examined your logic, someone else may have information or perspective that you are missing. Keep your mind open to the possibilities. Remember Rule 1: consider alternative explanations.

Bear in mind that seeking advice carries risks, but if you follow the rules and pay attention to the steps, you should be in a relatively protected position until the point at which you actually report your concerns officially. Note the caveats in these statements. As soon as you tell anyone else what worries you, you run the risk of losing control of the situation. Thus, proceed cautiously, but proceed all the same.

Remember also that the goal of the early steps is to collect enough information to decide whether you will be justified in making an official report of your concerns. At this point, you do not have enough information to know whether you should be filing such a report.

You are behaving professionally and responsibly to determine the appropriate future course.

To recap the rules for disputes at work:

Rule 1. Consider alternative explanations (especially that you may be wrong).

Rule 2. In light of Rule 1, ask questions; do not make charges.

Rule 3. Figure out what documentation supports your concerns and where it is.

Rule 4. Separate your personal and professional concerns.

Rule 5. Assess your goals.

Rule 6. Seek advice and listen to it.

How to Blow the Whistle and Still Have a Career Afterward

Let's say you've followed all the rules and believe you still must move forward to report suspected misconduct. Before moving into the steps, remember that how you conduct yourself will receive a disproportionate and maybe even unfair emphasis in the process. Here's why.

Good Faith and Malicious Charges

It's a rare situation in which the motivation of the whistle-blower isn't questioned at some point, so—once again—know who you are and where you stand. Think back to your report about Ben's cookie or setting a fire. The question of motive becomes a question of good faith. Good-faith reports must be protected—even when ultimately wrong about the facts. In contrast, people who make reports in bad faith or maliciously can be charged with misconduct themselves.

Filing mistaken charges when there was good reason to know they were false is the key element of most definitions of bad faith that could be subject to punishment or prosecution. It's in this context that lawyers sometimes ask whether the accuser "knew or should have known" from information readily available that the charges were false. Was it really you that took the cookie or started the fire? Saying that Ben did it when you did it yourself (or watched Alex do it) shows bad faith. On the other hand, if you saw Ben do it and had no way of knowing that Alex paid him to do it, say, or that Dad had given him permission to do it, you would likely have been acting in good faith, even if you were happy that Ben got into trouble. One key marker to watch for is adherence to professional standards of conduct; that is always strong evidence of good-faith behavior.

In general, the issue of good faith probably gets attention disproportionate to its importance because of how we feel about tattling. After all, if the facts reported are true, the motive of the whistle-blower should not matter. Even where the whistle-blower delights in the problems of the wrongdoer, if the evidence reveals that important professional or company standards were violated, the motives of the person raising the question should be irrelevant. Our general ambivalence about tattletales probably explains why motive is seldom considered irrelevant in practice. This reinforces your central dilemma: how can you conduct yourself so the question of your motives doesn't become the focus, rather than the acts that are worrying you?

While the existence of animosity does not in itself establish bad faith, it will affect how events unfold. Those who are experienced with receiving concerns about possible misconduct find a huge proportion of the cases involve personality conflicts or escalating political battles. They will almost always probe for evidence of bad blood between the players. Once working relationships become strained, trust erodes and likewise good will. Conduct that might have been accepted or explained away when people were on good terms with each other is perceived through a darker lens. Or the actions may not constitute actual misconduct yet may well be inappropriate (abuse or misuse of power, bullying or intimidation of subordinates, etc.). It helps to have established the kind of professional persona where the question of your motives doesn't overpower the issues. So if the person receiving the allegations asks about problems between the principals, that is not to explain away or excuse fraudulent behavior; the questions are designed to gain a fuller understanding of what might be going on, to understand both sides of the story.

You've prepared as best you can. Now it's time to move forward with filing your charges.

Procedures for Responsible Whistle-Blowing

Step 1: Review Your Concerns with
Someone You Trust

Talk quietly and confidentially with someone you trust who is in a position to evaluate your concerns and, if possible, is in a position of equal or greater power than the person whose conduct is at issue for you. His or her perspective may provide insights you do not have on your own; moreover, the relationship you form may provide the foundation for an alliance you may need going forward if the issue is not resolved through these early steps. Think about mentors you have had, professors who might be helpful, or someone you know through an internship. Think about respected professionals who are family friends. Follow Rules 1 and 2 above very carefully. Ask questions (only); do not lodge charges. Explain what concerns you and ask for help understanding the situation.

It is usually not a good idea to talk with many of your peers about your concerns. First, people at your level are likely to share the disadvantage of limited access to information. Second, if word spreads—and it likely will—that you're questioning the conduct of, and gossiping (which is how the talk will be perceived) about your boss, it will not reflect well on you. There are times when the power of the group can help to get a practice changed, and you're unlikely to harness it by spreading your concerns around before you've found the right, informed, and trustworthy sounding board. Be very careful whom you choose and what you confide. (Members of your family cannot be expected to understand the work context, and they might also lean to taking your side of the story when rendering advice.)

Before you get into the substance of your concerns with the person from whom you seek advice, confirm if he or she is in a position to be able to protect your confidences. Some people, because of their positions (e.g., compliance responsibilities carrying mandatory reporting obligations, say) or personal situations (maybe even a close relationship with the person you're concerned about), may not be able to promise confidentiality. If such a pledge is not possible, go elsewhere or seek a pledge to notify you before any revelations are made, and to protect you to the greatest possible extent.

As difficult as it may be, focus on facts at all times, not your feelings about the person whose conduct concerns you. Those feelings may need to be addressed, but they do not affect the substantive issues at the root of your concerns.

All along, keep refining the elements of the information you present to make as coherent and logical a presentation as possible: how your concerns first arose, what you did to assess them and/or to seek out alternative explanations, whom you have consulted to date, the advice you received, and what you did in response to that advice. You should be able to indicate what evidence is relevant to your concerns and where it can be found.

In a business context, you might say: "In training, we were instructed that only current-quarter completed sales could be included in our reports. I was told to book several sales that, as far as I can tell from the contracts I've processed, are not yet complete. When I asked Ms. Jones about this, she told me not to ask questions and to go ahead and include them. I understand that I'm pretty far down the food chain here. Maybe there are procedures I'm too new to know about or my training doesn't apply here. Can you help me figure out what I should do? The booked contracts are all recorded in the system. Can you help me understand how it works? Do I need to go back and brush up on my procedures?"

In the research setting, it might go like this: "I first became concerned when I noticed that the figures in the paper didn't match data I collected. When I asked Dr. Smith about it, I was told that these data came from one of our collaborators who used a more precise instrument than we have available. The thing that worries me is that

I used such an instrument in my previous lab, and its output doesn't resemble what is presented. When I asked about this, I was told it wasn't my concern. I consulted Dr. Deliberate, who's an expert on this instrument. She confirmed that no version of the instrument could produce data in this form. I am very confused and am trying to figure out an appropriate way to proceed. Can you help me figure out what to do? I've been told explicitly not to ask more questions in my lab. On the other hand, I'm worried that a miscommunication may be leading to problems. The data I collected are in my notebook on the third shelf from the left in Room 697. I've brought copies of those as well as a copy of the version of the manuscript that first led to my concerns and some literature Dr. Deliberate gave me describing the features of the instrument I was told produced the data in figures 4 and 7. What is your advice?"

Step 2: Listen to What That Person Tells You

If your chosen consultant disagrees with your perspective or discourages you from pursuing your questions, try with all your might to evaluate that response objectively. Do not assume he or she is trying to protect someone else or is simply a coward. Consider carefully the possibility that you are just plain wrong in your suspicions. Then, review the conversation to determine whether the consultant's position is character-based ("I know Ruth Jones and she would never do that") or fact-based ("Based on my experience with x, y, and z, that seems unlikely to me for the following reasons . . ."). If it is the latter and you cannot rebut one set of facts with another, you will have reason to reassess your conclusions.

If, however, the consultant does agree that there may be a problem, he or she might be willing to carry the charges personally. And if that person's status is equal to or greater than that of the person whose conduct you're questioning, that could be invaluable. Or perhaps that person—or someone you consult for a second opinion—will join you in filing a statement of concern with the appropriate authorities. You can explore the possibility that others in your environment who are experiencing the same problem might also join you in making a report or asking that the questions you raise are examined.

If you're still uncertain about what to do, apply Step 3, with care.

Step 3: Get a Second Opinion and Take That Seriously, Too

Bear in mind before taking this step that most communities are relatively small and that word travels within them. Your actions may well arouse the rumor mill or grapevine, which can be damaging. Your demeanor in the process thus becomes all the more crucial. All the advice from Step 1 applies here. Ask questions and stay focused on facts. Be careful to verify that the person you consult can provide you with confidential, personal advice and monitor the professional quality of how you present yourself and your motives at all times.

Again, assess the response you receive very carefully, as in Step 2. Does any aspect of it change your perception of the situation? Can you rebut that information with other facts, not just your conviction that Dr. Smith is a slippery character who is not to be trusted?

Go back and apply all the rules and reassess where you stand. If you believe that going forward is the right thing to do, work through Step 4 carefully and thoroughly.

Step 4: Seek Strength in Numbers

Inquire whether those you consulted will join you in filing a statement of concern with the appropriate authorities. Are there others in your environment who are experiencing the same problem or who may have observed the same actions that cause you concern? Listen carefully to see if others are expressing the same views. Do so carefully: do not charge in heedlessly. Every additional person with whom you speak forthrightly increases the possibility that you will catalyze the rumor mill. This increases the chance that word will get back to the person whose conduct concerns you in (usually) the most damaging possible way for you. Thus, take special care to stick to the advice in the rules and continue to ask questions in a way that holds open the possibility that you are mistaken. If it seems prudent and feasible, see if those who are concerned will combine with you in making a report of your concerns or of asking that someone look into the questions you raise. If the response is negative, try to figure out their reasons: Do they disagree with you? Do they agree but think the matter is not important enough to pursue or that another approach would be more constructive? Do they fear the consequences? Some of these considerations are more important than others for you to factor into your ultimate decision. Regardless, continue to take special care to proceed in a way that holds open the chance that you are mistaken.

This can be a lonely business, and having support may mean the difference between surviving the process with a career intact and not. Better, even if all you get from your contacts is moral support, that will count, and it will help; if your efforts result in the formation of a group of people committed to present charges together, better still. Is there an ombudsperson, ethics hotline, or victim advocate you can call? Any steps you can take to reduce or prevent your isolation will be a gain.

Step 5: Find the Right Place to File
Charges; Study the Procedures

You'll be setting yourself up for disappointment if you seek recourse from a body that has no authority to look into your questions or no legitimate connection to the work you question. (For example, professional societies and journal editors—though frequently asked to investigate claims made in papers submitted to them—usually lack the resources to do much direct investigation, being dependent instead upon the home institutions of the researchers.)

Ascertain whether there is a relationship between the person whose conduct concerns you and the organization to which you will be reporting. Know the organization's oversight process and work on getting some leverage through it, because it may be necessary to alert that oversight point when you formally invoke an organization's procedures so you can ensure that your charges do not get lost, accidentally or on purpose.

Know before you take your first formal steps what procedures will be followed. Corporations have internal ethics and compliance offices, and those offices will have information about the rules and how to access their systems. Institutions receiving federal research funds are required to have written policies. Get a copy of the relevant policies or rules and read them. Look for information on the following topics:

- Are you required to submit your charges in writing, or can it be done orally?
- Who will be informed of the charges you make?
- What role will you have in the process?
- What safeguards will be applied to protect against conflicts of interest among those reviewing the matters you are raising?
- Who will be informed of the outcome of the process? How will that occur?

The answers to these questions will not necessarily change your next step; they will prepare you for the process and minimize any unpleasant surprises. If, after exploring all the issues thoroughly, you conclude that your concerns are well founded and the matter is serious enough, then—and only then—proceed to Step 6.

Step 6: Report Your Concerns

To the maximum extent possible, continue to pose your concerns neutrally or in the form of questions. Remember that you still are not asserting that "Director Plum is inflating sales numbers" or "Dr. Mustard is committing scientific fraud." You are stating facts, asking questions, or raising concerns along with specific information about how those concerns may be assessed. The tone will be something like this: "The reported sales figures shown in data files 93-406 seem discrepant from the division's reports," or "The published data from three experiments conducted between June and December 2009 appear to differ from those in the laboratory books kept in the blue cupboard on the east wall of room 2546," or "The first two sections of the paper published by Dr. Scarlet seem to track my dissertation very closely. I am not listed as an author on the paper."

No matter how careful you have been in following the rules and procedures for responsible whistle-blowing, there may be facts of which you are unaware that make the situation dramatically different from your current perception of it. Your interests will be better served in the long run if you can avoid attaching labels, attributing motives, or displaying venom in your interactions.

When you make your report, provide all the documentation you can and all the information about its location that you have.

Step 7: Ask Questions; Keep Notes

If there is a meeting at which you report your concerns, ask questions and keep careful notes of the answers you are given. Date your notes and record who was present when you were provided with each item of information. Ask what steps will follow and to what extent you will be kept informed. Ask if there is someone whom you may call or who will contact you regularly to keep you apprised of the status of the situation. Will you be called to testify in the process? Given an opportunity to respond to information presented about your concerns? Informed when the process is over?

If you are interviewed by a company lawyer or called to testify before an investigating committee, find out if you may be accompanied by a friend or advisor, for moral support if nothing else. These occasions can be stressful, and you may not hear or remember things as well on your own as you would otherwise. A trusted person can call for a break to help you regain your composure if you get wrapped up in the emotions of the moment, and after the meeting can help you form a balanced perspective about it.

Under ordinary circumstances, you shouldn't need to engage an attorney; if you do, it may send signals that are counterproductive. However, it is wise to have someone accompany you who puts your interests first, hears all that is said, and can help you assess how the process is functioning. Note that advance legal advice may help protect you in some circumstances. If there is no one you can consult confidentially inside the company or university, or if the conduct that concerns you is very serious if true (such as criminal conduct or serious financial irregularities), you may want some legal advice before you begin. If the university or company has received publicity for treating previous whistle-blowers very badly, or for responding to problems with all-out attempts to whitewash, you may want to arm yourself with good legal advice in advance. It still may not be a good idea to be accompanied by an attorney when you file your charges, but having an effective lawyer on your side and knowing your legal position before taking action is sometimes a wise precaution. A caution: unless the attorney is experienced or knowledgeable in the specific area of your complaint, the advice may not be of much use to you. Do some networking to find the right lawyer. Contact one of the whistle-blower support organizations or a successful whistle-blower for a referral to an appropriate attorney.

Overall, focus on big-picture objectives and avoid slurs on character. Try to project a calm, nonvindictive demeanor: Your feelings should not be the focus of these proceedings; the factual matters in question should be. Once again, take all of your documentation and notes and be prepared to provide copies if you have not done so previously.

Keep your advisors and advocates informed and try to keep a sense of humor and perspective. Find ways to work off the frustrations that will inevitably arise. Get personal support outside the process.

Step 8: Cultivate Patience

This process always takes longer than will feel reasonable. If there is a formal inquiry or investigation, it is likely to be conducted by more than one person, or even by a committee. The logical problems of getting together and communicating with a number of busy people can impede rapid progress, even before any other complexities arise. It is important not to make assumptions about what is happening or what it might mean and to remain in periodic contact with the person to whom you reported your concerns. Be patient, persistent, and professional. Always follow the rules in how you conduct yourself.

To recap the procedures for responsible whistle-blowing:

1. Review your concerns with someone you trust.
2. Listen to what that person tells you.
3. Get a second opinion and take that seriously, too.
4. If you decide to initiate formal proceedings, seek strength in numbers.
5. Find the right place to file charges; study the procedures.
6. Report your concerns.
7. Ask questions; keep notes.
8. Cultivate patience.

Conclusion

It is possible to blow the whistle and still have a career afterward, and it takes a combination of common sense, prudence, and some luck. If you have followed these rules and steps carefully, you have done a great deal to protect yourself as you move through an investigation of suspected misconduct. There are no guarantees; following these steps should leave you reasonably well informed and help you to make good decisions.

Such proceedings are difficult for everyone involved. By following these rules, you should be able to maximize the likelihood that questions that concern you are serious ones deserving concentrated review. In the process, by moving cautiously and step by step, you will minimize some of the worst consequences that can happen to whistle-blowers and still have a productive career with your good name intact.

A Separate Note: If You Are Wrongly Accused

1. Have good manners. Be polite and respectful to everyone. Your greatest asset as you go through any difficult personal and professional experience is the goodwill of others toward you. You want people to like and respect you.

2. Stay calm and also make it clear that there must be some error and that you have not committed misconduct. If there has been a mistake, you need to state so from the beginning while being as professional in your demeanor as possible. Make it clear to all that you want a full examination of the relevant facts because no one is more interested than you are in your good name and in clearing up the mistaken accusations.

3. Ask questions—a lot of them. How did this problem arise? Where did it come from? Who are the players? What is the timeline? When and how will you be contacted next? Who should you contact if you have questions? What are your rights?

4. Be introspective. Figure out what specific acts or behavior might have led to this situation. Focus on actions you and others took. It will not help to attribute motives to others. While this can be a natural impulse, avoid it to the maximum extent possible.

5. Take responsibility. Recognize any of your actions that might have contributed to the situation and figure out how to talk about them in a calm and collected way.

6. Gather documentation. Make copies of the relevant records, if you can, and assure they're in a safe place. Consider applicable rules as you do so and weigh the risks of setting yourself up for charges of theft or interference with ongoing work. Ask to examine all materials being used against you.

This might be a good place to talk about the importance of always keeping good records, which is at the base of good research and business practices. Carelessness or sloppiness can cause enormous problems and even charges of misconduct. In contrast, meticulous records can resolve questions and cause misplaced allegations to be dismissed before they morph into a large and unpleasant investigation.

Make sure the entire process is well documented. The worst thing that can happen to you is for the matter to be handled informally, yet rumors dog you for the rest of your career.

CHAPTER 6

Stay on the High Road

And End Up Where You Mean to Be

Traveling the high road means playing a long game, looking at your life over a longer arc than just the part you're currently inhabiting. It means that you understand that what goes around, comes around (even though it often takes longer than feels just). When you choose the high road, you consider your actions in terms of how each one will accumulate and contribute to or detract from the reputation you hope to hold at the end of your career.

You try to live life consistently according to your values, not just when it's easy or convenient. You choose people with whom to associate and organizations with which to affiliate that will reinforce and support those values.

You respect the humanity of individuals you meet and accord courtesy to all, regardless of status or what each might do for you. You separate, as much as you can, personalities and how much you like people from your assessments of their contributions.

You understand that it's easy to form judgments and make choices based on factors that might not stand up to close examination, and you build checks and balances into your decision-making process to prevent that.

As much as you can, by building good career habits and understanding how things go wrong, you prepare for the realities of a world in which the values of others may not always match your own. You pause before reacting to perceived affronts by rising above the instinct to retaliate and by following the rules for conducting a dispute professionally.

You avoid the mistakes you can and insulate yourself from predictable pressures. When you make choices in your life, and even mistakes, you are willing to take responsibility for them and their consequences.

While the high road may at times seem like a longer, harder, and bumpier journey, there are processes and perspectives that will support and empower you along the way. Soliciting and welcoming feedback is one such. In addition to gathering information, it engenders respect, builds in reciprocity, and averts surprises.

Solicit and Welcome Feedback

Others see us more clearly than we see ourselves. What employees think of their job and social skills, for example, correlates with what peers think of them only a third of the time.[1] Assessment by peers is twice as likely to agree with the assessment of supervisors as with our assessments of ourselves.[2] There's important information to be had from others, and it is not always easy to ask for or to hear. Or, surprisingly, even to obtain: Getting constructive feedback in the world of work is harder than you'd think.

In his recollection of his career, Sir Peter Medawar, a Nobel Prize–winning scientist, gives us a clue to the reluctance of even a very senior professional to criticize a junior colleague. Medawar was present when an outright scientific fraud was being presented as fact. Medawar recognized the fraud, in real time, for what it was, and yet he didn't speak up. "I simply lacked the moral courage to say at the time that I thought we were the victims of a hoax or confidence trick. It is easy in theory to say these things, but in practice very senior scientists do not like trampling on their juniors in public."[3] If someone at the pinnacle of career power felt uncomfortable speaking out in the face of an obvious hoax, we can see how hard it can be to come by feedback in a normal professional context.

The world is full, even overfull, of managers who aren't comfortable specifying their expectations or providing constructive evaluations to those who work for them, especially to people they like (which isn't to say there aren't managers completely at ease ripping into you in front of others—that's a different animal). Many people don't understand that it's possible to be direct without being brutal and that it doesn't spare anyone to skip the hard parts hoping they'll be divined or guessed. Much of the work I do with managers and leaders is devoted to helping them understand that setting guidelines and providing candid feedback benefits everyone, and then teaching the skills to do it well. It's a surprisingly hard sell, because it's so uncomfortable to have conversations that tell someone face to face, "This specific aspect of what you're doing is a problem and must change in this way."

A manager worried that one of his key technical analysts was alienating customers, sought coaching to help him construct a script that included instances of inappropriate conduct, along with expectations for how to improve. Rather than simply saying, "You were impossible this morning," he learned to be more specific: "When you spoke over the client's VP while she was still responding to your question, it caused her to wonder if we are right for this job. Her perspective on the problem is different from yours. It is our job to understand her view. In this instance, you did not have all of the facts before you spoke. I expect you not to interrupt when the client is speaking and to take notes, demonstrating respect and comprehension of the information she is conveying to us."

If you're not getting information about your supervisor's expectations, especially when you sense unhappiness with your work, your future may be determined by how you react.

An unfortunately common pattern, which all too often leads to grievances or lawsuits, is the supervisor who is unhappy with a subordinate and does not say so. The employee gets no negative feedback and therefore no chance to improve. One day, the supervisor erupts from accumulated (unexpressed) frustration and fires the employee, who's usually stunned because his file is full of positive evaluations, even commendations and awards. This failure to provide feedback before termination provides job security for a lot of human resources people and lawyers in cases where there's no documentation or appropriate procedures weren't followed.

All of this explains why expensive leadership development programs and corporate leadership tracks often include 360-degree evaluations. (These evaluations seek information about your performance from your supervisors, your peers, and the people who report to you.) Their aim is to help overcome the cringe factor that poses so many obstacles to getting needed information.

You can create your own feedback system to avoid becoming one of those surprised fired people by taking Peter Drucker's advice to learn to manage yourself. Since in virtually every dispute both parties play a role in how a situation develops, you want to be able to assess the part you play and the responsibility you share. Indicating your openness to concerns is, by itself, a strong signal to team members that you want to have constructive working relationships with them. I recommend adding a fourth element to Drucker's three-step contribution conversation, introduced in Chapter 2, for starting healthy working relationships: an element to deal clearly with problems. You could say something like, "If I am not meeting your expectations or you are disappointed in something I've done, I would appreciate knowing about it," and then, with coworkers, make the invitation reciprocal: "How would you like me to signal you if I am worried about your portion of the project?"[4]

To correct problems before they become too big to fix, focus on helping others overcome their inhibitions about providing the information you need. To demonstrate your commitment to having the information, you may have to cultivate a thick skin and nondefensive posture. Your script for responding to information about your work that hurts or surprises you will be especially important. A quiet "thank you for this information; I care about doing a good job," can be very effective.

Structuring a reciprocal way to solicit and provide feedback can be off-putting and you may flip into avoidance mode. Remember that having a chance to improve while you're still on the job is better than the surprise firing. Still, it can be daunting, especially since once you seek out the information, you're not done: you must also receive it professionally. If you react angrily or defensively the first time someone responds to your invitation for feedback, it may be the last time too, because you will have shut down future efforts.

Hold yourself still, focus on listening and aim to be nonreactive. Ask questions to make sure you fully understand what's being said and where it's coming from; if the views you're hearing are based on misinformation or misunderstandings, you can address the inaccuracies later after you've had a chance to consider the entire situation in private, including processing your emotional reaction, and to construct a script for opening a constructive conversation. Hold onto the thought that you cannot correct misimpressions or misunderstandings without knowing what others are thinking.

No one has more invested in your own growth than you do.

A supervisor responding to a grievance from a fired employee couldn't understand why the grievance was even being considered since the employee had a high absence rate and was chronically tardy. The employee felt betrayed. A mother of young children who was also caring for an aged parent, she'd described the problems with her unreliable transportation, explained when her parent's health crises kept her away, and worked hard to complete her assigned projects on time. Each time she had been absent or late, she had checked in with the supervisor, who had sympathized, said he understood, and told her he appreciated her efforts to communicate and cover the work. Because he was soothing and kind when she was late, the employee assumed that everything was okay. The supervisor, though he liked the employee personally, was fuming inside, feeling that his good will was being abused. He thought "everyone should know" that coming to work regularly, and on time, was a baseline requirement. He'd never said out loud what his expectations were or provided any written warnings (as the personnel policy required), nor had he consulted human resources. Had he done so, he could have been helped to formulate a script with clear declarative sentences laying out expectations and what would flow from not meeting them. He would have protected himself from the hassle of the grievance and the employee from the shock of termination.

Mindreading is a very imperfect form of communication.

When I was on a school board long ago, we hired a new superintendent. In his interview, he said he would like to have quarterly feedback from each board member, on a continuing basis. It was an unexpected request because annual evaluations are more common and are normally pretty dry, rote procedures. Once we started the practice, novel to each of us, our board members valued it tremendously and so did our superintendent. Once we learned that he was serious about seeking both positive feedback and suggestions for how things could be working better, the practice kept the lines of communication open and reduced surprises. He served as superintendent for twelve years, when the average national tenure for school superintendents is closer to three or four. His success and longevity were directly related to the fact that he sought and listened to feedback regularly and structured a way to provide information to those evaluating him about the context and choices he was making.

Understanding Conflicts, Veracity, and Transparency

Use what you've learned so far to help you preempt mistakes and reduce friction in your working life. Add onto that by adopting three more habits to help you avoid errors of judgment and rise above other predictable problems: recognize conflicting loyalties, practice veracity, and strive for transparency.

Identify Conflicting Loyalties

Handling conflicts of loyalties and observing or experiencing conflicts of interest (no, they are not the same) are challenges you'll face repeatedly as you make your way through your organization.

They can throw you off balance as they test your personal standards. Conflicts of interest are generally considered in the financial or personal career realm, as when you or someone in your family or circle of intimacy might financially benefit, like the purchasing agent buying from his nephew's company. Conflicts of loyalties is a broader concept, covering more than just financial interests.

Your Friend's Future

One of your friends who works on a project overseen by your boss has asked you for advice about her future with your corporation. She has received an attractive job offer that involves a promotion. You know that the vice president of your division has decided to end this project in six months and then your friend and everyone else will be out of work. You are under strict instructions not to tell anyone because the entire team is needed through completion of this phase to deliver on time.

Telling your friend the truth about her soon-to-be-terminated project will be best for her, both personally and professionally. On the other hand, doing so will violate direct instructions from your boss, costing you his trust if he finds out. Whether he finds out or not, if you do it you will know you broke faith with your professional obligation of confidentiality. If you don't do it, you will be breaking faith with your friend, your self-image, and your personal identity.

This is a problem of conflicting loyalties—to your friend and to the requirements of your job. It's not just a problem of the moment: Situations like it will recur throughout your professional life. Do you have options? Are you willing to live with the consequences of each? Sure, you could just tell your friend, swear her to silence, and hope no one ever finds out. Even if that best-hope scenario plays out, though, both you and she now know you will violate professional confidences under some circumstances.

A crucial question is whether you are willing to counsel your friend that she should pass up the job to stay and complete the project. Is it the case that working on a completed project might advance her career opportunities more than taking a new, higher-level job now? Could you in good faith encourage your friend to stay on, saying it's better for her career, when you know it's not? Were your boss's instructions generic or would he actually want you to do that? If he would truly put the interests of a short-term project over the long-term career prospects of a good employee, what does that say about him and maybe the company? Doesn't that raise the stakes when those values are at odds with your own?

A middle course would be to tell your friend that you cannot give her advice. Non-advice advice ducks her direct question about her future with your corporation. Can you draw a boundary, saying you cannot discuss the corporation's future plans with her? Doing so might telegraph information without supplying it directly if you're not careful (essentially, "I cannot tell you about your future here because you don't have one"). Sending that message would violate the spirit, though not the letter, of your boss's instructions, so even the middle course might be a problem from his perspective and might threaten your own advancement if you're not careful.

If you value your friend more than your job, your loyalties might not be split and you would just advise her to take the new offer. Your self-regard and reputation for truthfulness would remain intact. Competing loyalties, however, are fundamentally boundary questions. If you have been scrupulous about professional boundaries from the beginning of your relationship, you could quite naturally tell your friend to do whatever she thinks best for her career (like the lawyer in my class on negotiation who said, "That's not a question I'm going to answer—you know that").

Boundary violations trip up a lot of new supervisors; navigating them is a special challenge when you assume authority over people with whom you might once have been peers or friends or over people older than you are.

Covering for Your Friend

Managing a team with a close friend on it, I became aware that the friend was interviewing for other jobs and missing interim deadlines. My friend asked me to cover for her with the promise that she would meet the final goal date, but as it neared, her work wasn't completed. I was responsible for providing my boss with an accurate picture of our progress and also wanted to protect my friend's reputation.

As team manager, you have not done your friend any favors by letting the deadlines slide and not speaking to her about the problem. Just as you would want to hear first if you were not meeting expectations, it is your responsibility to speak clearly to your friend—early, rather than later—about work problems so she can correct them. If you have mastered the dynamics of feedback as you have moved through your career, you should be prepared to provide it. If you had spoken with her when the first deadline was missed, you wouldn't be in a such a big hole now. Doing the work at work and keeping the friendship separate would have served both of you better.

Respect Truth—and Consequences

Remember grandma and the question of lying about the itchy, ugly sweater? Adopting a policy about truthfulness and about what you will and will not say is an important matter to think through, particularly as it surfaces in your work life. A large component of your reputation will grow out of your coworkers' observations of how well you keep confidences and how much your word can be trusted.

There's a difference, as with grandma, in saying every thought that comes to mind (Itchy! Scratchy!) and sorting through what you can say that is truthful and still not cruel (the sweater makes you feel loved). If your close friend asks you whether she looks fat in her dress, neither of you wants you to say, "Actually, you do look kinda like the side of a barn." Finding a line between impolitic truths and being deceptive can be tricky, and each of us must grapple with that. What matches your own comfort level and self-image?

For example, if you are selling a TV, few people would find it ethical to say yes in response to the question, "Is it in working condition?" if it wasn't working at all. On the other hand, if you answer, "The last time I had it on, it was working perfectly," some people would consider it the responsibility of the buyer to pick up on the hedge in the answer and ask how long ago that was, or whether anything has happened to the TV since the last time it was on. A good test is whether you would be willing to say things to people's faces. There's some evidence that we are more likely to lie on the telephone and in e-mail than we are in person.[5] Another test is how you would feel about being caught in the contradiction or prevarication.

To complicate matters even more, we have different rules for different settings. It would be much less acceptable to play word games about the TV's condition if you were selling it to a friend or relative. You might say one thing to your friend about her dress if you're in the store trying it on and something else if she asks as you're both entering the ballroom for a big event. In the first case, you might find a way to say, "I think that other one flattered you more," and in the second, when there's nothing she can do about it anyway, something reassuring—and still you can do it without lying.

In professional settings, there are some very hard lines: It is never acceptable in the United States to lie to a judge in a courtroom, or to a federal agent—remember Martha Stewart? Your corporate culture will determine a lot about the tolerance for fuzziness and will likely influence you without your awareness if you haven't thought all these issues through in advance. But if your nosy neighbor asks a question about your personal life that is none of her business, it's usually considered acceptable (and maybe sensible) to deflect the question or even to tell only a partial version of the truth. Of course, if you have the wherewithal to find a nice way to say, "That's none of your business," like the lawyer who wouldn't answer a question in a negotiation, that's even better.

Being a truth teller can be complicated by issues of conflicting loyalties. As in the case of the friend seeking career advice, you may have professional information you cannot share, even when it is true, and even when it could help you or others. Imagine that you have access through your job to privileged information about a company's plans that would permit you to make a lot of money if you were to act on it before it becomes public. If you do this in publicly traded securities, you might just have committed the federal crime of insider trading.

But what if you don't plan to make money off the information, just protect someone?

Your Widowed Aunt's Investments

You are a summer intern for a local accountant. At a family dinner, your recently widowed aunt talks about her plan to invest all of your uncle's estate in the company he worked for, since he was a lifelong employee and they treated him very well. This money is her main asset. A few weeks ago, you noticed a pattern of the largest local clients moving their money out of the company, which is the area's major employer. You asked your boss about it and he said there were serious concerns about the company's viability, so all those in the know were moving their money before the company goes under. He tells you this is confidential, company-private information, and you cannot disclose it. What do you do?

This dilemma wasn't an insider trading problem, but it did squarely present serious conflicts of loyalty. Accountants have professional obligations to protect client financial data, yet letting your aunt pour all her money into a rat-hole is unthinkable. If you cannot tell the truth, is there an honorable way to steer her off her determined course—like suggesting that a diversified portfolio is a smarter way to go and you'd be happy to help her develop one, or striving to slow down her process until decisive news emerges publicly? Variations on this dilemma arise regularly in professional life. When they come up, they will test you, and advance preparation can help you be true to your values and loyalties.

Consider the situation of two lawyers in Illinois who endured an agonizing experience, in which a client they were representing on an unrelated matter told them he'd committed a murder for which someone else was in jail. He even signed a formal confession—and refused to permit them to reveal it. Legal ethics, similar to medical ethics, required them to keep their client's confidence, even as someone else was suffering for it. The two lawyers consulted state ethics boards, other lawyers, and judges, trying to find a way they could, within the understood bounds of their professional ethics, be released from their obligation to keep the client's confidence so they could help the unjustly imprisoned man. At every turn, they were told to stay quiet. The two kept the signed confession in their safe for twenty-six years, having secured their client's permission to release it after his death. To reveal the confidence would have meant giving up being lawyers, as they could have been disbarred and lost their licenses to practice law. People inside and outside the legal profession have argued about the ethics of this case then and ever since. Is this a case of two competing rights (maintaining client confidentiality vs. overturning an unjust conviction) or is it a larger question, of something else entirely?[6]

It can be hard to stay on the high road when challenged to act or react when the issue is how much of what you know to share, especially when you are bumping into professional boundaries. In the case of a family doctor faced with a choice between the protection of her professional license and the survival of a child, it's tough even to discern which road is the high road.[7] Imagine that you are this doctor. Your patient asks you to lie to shield him from having to admit to his wife that he has not been tested for compatibility as a kidney donor for their daughter because his paralyzing surgery phobia means he couldn't be a donor even if he were a match. He absolutely does not want his wife to know that he hasn't been tested. She's in the waiting room and he wants you to call her in and tell her he has been tested and isn't a match. You have a professional obligation, backed up by federal law, to respect his medical privacy. What do you do? Why? How?

Would it influence your view if he were not the dad but instead a fourth cousin, or if he were not related at all? It probably would, because part of what's coloring the picture are your feelings about the obligation a father owes his child. How much does it color your perspective on your professional obligation that you know a seven-year-old could die without your taking action? What kind of actions do you consider? How do you deal with the father's request that you lie?

Are you willing to go out and tell the mother he's not a match? Most people would not be willing, recognizing that a direct lie goes beyond a doctor's obligation to a patient. What if the dad asks you just to say, "We do not have a donor"? That is a completely true statement: since he's not willing to be tested, you do not have a donor. Most people would quickly conclude that is a lie by omission, and one the physician shouldn't tell. A workable definition of a lie is that it (a) is intended to deceive, and (b) does deceive, the listener. (That's a useful test, by the way, for choosing words at work: if you intend to deceive and succeed, chances are high that you have told a lie.)

What if the father asks you only to stand beside him in your white coat while he tells the mother he's not a match? Are you willing just to do that? Why or why not? Most of those with whom I've discussed this over the years would not be willing do that either, because it adds authority by implication to the lie the father is telling. But what if he doesn't directly say he's not a match and instead himself says, "We do not have a donor?"

Still uncomfortable? What are you going to do? One choice is to send him out alone and do nothing.

At the other end of the spectrum, are you willing to violate your professional commitment to patient confidentiality and tell his wife he hasn't been tested? You'd be telling the truth, possibly helping to save a life (and maybe fracturing a family in the process), and you'd be violating professional and legal boundaries that proscribe the sharing of that information.

In the middle, what problem-solving resources and options can you access to help you persuade this man that his fear is misplaced? Could you call in the hospital social workers? The ethics committee? Would you spend your own time exploring his fears and trying to assuage them? Might you move things forward if you try to persuade him to get tested by pointing out that he might well not be a match at all and so would never even have to face pressure from the family?

At the end of the day, if he won't budge and you cannot find a donor, are you willing to stand by and watch the child die? Is this your decision?

There are instances when many of us will decide to violate laws or regulations when we believe they are wrong; the entire principle of civil disobedience, for example, is premised on that idea. The rule with such choices is that you must be willing to bear the consequences of your action, which in this case, depending on the jurisdiction, could lead to your paying a fine, being suspended, or even losing your practice privileges or professional license.

In many, if less harrowing, professional messes, how you approach and manage interactions from the beginning might head off problems. Even in this situation, might you have built your relationship with the father as your patient differently or with clearer signals? Had you known about his surgery phobia? For how long? Did you ever talk about it together? Were there any aspects of your initial establishment of the boundaries in your relationship or in the professional persona you presented that could have given him the idea you'd participate in his scheme? Were you diligent enough in setting out a methodical program of family testing and documentation or setting out the ground rules of how it would all work? Seeking clarity and permissions for who would be told what? This is such a fraught situation that it is not clear that any of those actions could have made a difference, but they might have.

Did you start as you meant to go on?

Practice Values Transparency

People draw their lines in different places to determine what falls within their personal boundaries and sense of integrity. That doesn't mean there isn't any right and wrong; it means that experience, training, background, and character bring people to different answers. Some people's answers are going to be far beyond your—or my—limits. Like the student who aspired to be a "ruthless winner" and the boss who told the intern not to be such a girl scout about posing as a customer to collect information from competitors, there are those who will do whatever they can get away with.

And then there are those who play by a consistent set of rules, who practice transparency, such that people are able to decide responsibly whether to work or do business with them. My friend David owns a start-up company. He sees sales tactics daily that he considers over the line: situations in which the company's purchasing agent receives personal benefits—a fancy meal, a gift card, attendance at a high-end sporting event, or an iPad—for listening to a sales pitch. In his enterprise, he makes it clear that if a vendor provides something in exchange for purchases, it belongs to the company, not to the person who places the order. He applies this procedure for purchases his company makes and in his sales policies as well.

That doesn't help much when the agent making a decision about buying his product for a large potential customer says to him, as one did once, "I'm a big scuba diver. The guy from your competitor is getting me a regulator for Christmas. I sure could use some tanks." In David's view, that's an outright bribe, and inappropriate. Does he walk away from the business to protect his scruples? Or, citing his company's strict polices, should he ask for written verification from the purchasing agent (and maybe his boss) that personal gifts don't violate that company's code of conduct? Is there another solution?

The world of sales, especially on commission, constantly presents dilemmas of "sweeteners" and "inducements," even in companies where the rules are strict, so preparing in advance is critical. One young professional reported immediately, as required by her company's business conduct guidelines, when she witnessed one of her competitors bribing a potential client. She wrote, "My manager surprised me. He wanted to know if it would be possible for us to prepare similar gifts, because our group needed more revenue and better sales results."

That young professional declined to do it and suffered almost immediate effects in her performance evaluations; she also raised the issue with a different employee of the client company, whose own corporate standards were violated by what she'd seen. What goes around comes around, though, and several years later, she was offered (and accepted) a job with the client company. They had noted her rectitude in dealing with the bribery event, and recruited her as a person they wanted on their team.

When the other guy's conduct implicates you and your own values, do you maintain your standards all the time, or only selectively (when it doesn't cost you very much)? That's a decision you must make early on, and keep making, as you make your way through the world of work—whether you're an entrepreneur who sets the rules or are subject to those made by others.

You may find yourself debating these issues internally, as well as with others.

Include Late Submission?

Your company has monthly deadlines for sales competition credits. One of the sales managers who reports to you missed his mandatory deadline for processing a large deal, which puts his whole team at risk for losing a chance at a bonus. He asks you to include that sale in their totals anyway when you report credits.

Why not do it? Why penalize his whole team for a small mistake by their leader? If the sales manager has never missed a deadline before, especially if you like him, this could seem to be a no-brainer. The deadline is arbitrary anyway, and the harm seems small.

So you decide to include the deal in the period's report—but not to hide what you're doing. Practicing transparency after making the requested exception would first mean telling the sales manager you'll be letting all the teams in the competition know about it.

Then it would mean telling the teams who met the deadline what you did. How will they feel about the sale being included in the competition?

However you explain it to yourself, a clear-sighted professional decision encompasses the realization that your choice may look different to other people, from your boss to corporate auditors. If you are comfortable explaining the choice and are willing to have it factored into your reputation, go for it. Just don't get sucked into making a self-serving choice without stepping back and considering the full consequences of your choices.

High-Road Go-To Solutions

These two approaches will come in handy at the beginning of your career, in the middle, and at the end.

Get It in Writing

The single most effective response to being asked to do something that makes you uncomfortable is to ask the boss to put the orders in writing.

If you ask in a low-key, nonconfrontational way, the results can be surprisingly positive. In the best of all possible worlds, deploying the right script for asking the boss to put the order in writing may give that person a moment to rethink and change his or her mind. Aim to avoid being aggressive or escalating the situation. Remain low key, calm, and matter of fact throughout. Even if the boss persists with the orders that trouble you, you'll have the written directions and whatever you do next, the paper trail will be clear about where the concept originated. You may not be off the hook, as you cannot defer your own values to those of others, but you're still better off than if you're the only one whose prints are on any part of the paper trail.

Remember the boss's travel reimbursement? In that case, my friend offered to provide the form for certifying that receipts had been lost and quietly indicated that she stood ready to do her part as soon as the required documentation—either receipts or the form—was provided.

It's possible, of course, that the boss will simply order you to do it and stop quibbling. Some things to try if you sense things are heating up are to take the dispute to a different setting, and to ask via e-mail for the documentation so there is a complete record all the way along of your requests and the responses.

If you didn't do that and you have it in you, ask again, or simply say quietly, "Of course. I'll send a confirming e-mail about our conversation," or "You really need this done quickly and I really want to do it in a way that protects you and the unit. I'll get help from audit [or the travel office or . . .] to make sure that once I send it through, it will stick." If you haven't escalated the situation through any aspect of your conduct, this will not necessarily be seen as a threat, though of course, at some level, it is. Your manner and tone can help prevent a serious aggression spiral. Your whole goal here is to project your most serious, calm, helpful, pleasant professional persona so there is nothing threatening in your manner.

Like a number of students, if you're facing the situation of being asked to initial documents you know to be wrong and pass them along to the next level, and the boss is insisting, you may have a harder problem: do it or report it. If your company has an ethics hotline, now might be a good time to call it. If you're the only possible source of the information and you have heard, via the grapevine, that the hotline is not confidential or effective, then you have a values-based decision to make about your next step. You could try to get the system changed, respectfully decline and deal with whatever comes next, or do something you feel is wrong.

Another option is to create a memo to the file (second cousin to the e-mail confirming the order) or some other form of documentation recording the bare facts. It's critical for your future that your memo contain facts only.

Now what if the "boss's mistake" is not just pressure, but an outright direction to break the law?

Just Sign Them—I Don't Care if You
Cannot Read Them!

You are overseeing transactions involving numerous documents. All the loan documents are in German, and no one in your office knows German. Your boss tells you just to sign off on the documents because it will cost too much to hire a translator; he is sure they are fine.

Remember first to ask questions. "I remember in my orientation session that they said specifically that we must fully understand every document we sign. Can you help me understand how this assignment follows that rule?" Or "I'm concerned that I will be exposing the company to problems if I sign something I cannot read. Is there someone I can ask about our liability?" Or "Could you put your request for me to process that in writing? If the auditors question this, I'd like to have the authority for the action in my records."

Eventually, you may need to state your position: "I can't sign my name to documents I cannot read." Remember that the how can matter as much as the what: the way you ask will be pivotal to the outcome. Strive to be respectful, nonconfrontational, and use a pleasant tone of voice.

The situation with the untranslated documents is not that far from what happened in many of the mortgage and foreclosure disasters of the recent economic crisis. More documents were being processed every day than anyone could (or did) ever read, so many mistakes were made that caused suffering and losses. In large systems with many essentially replaceable people (who, it must be noted, often make very large sums of money for their actions), the range of possible resistance to wrong acts can be very limited. In those bad situations, it's time to think about getting out, how to blow the whistle, or both. Of course, because the problem is not always what you think it is, it is wise to follow all the steps to have a dispute professionally and to blow the whistle before concluding that is the way to go.

Find Common Ground

If you seek out a negotiation workshop or do some reading on the topic, one of the first things you will learn is that successful persuasion is all about discovering and then addressing the other person's interests. Interests are the reasons people seek what they do and why they act the way they do. Surprisingly often, people have not thought all the way through their own interests in formulating their positions, and if you are dealing with someone in that state of mind, arguing or persuasion are not likely to be very effective. If you ask enough questions that you come to understand the person's interests, sometimes, along the way, he or she will discover the same thing, and it may affect the outcome in ways that are beneficial to both of you.

Take a fairly standard conflict that occurs between departments that have a history of friction. One passes data to the other, which then incorporates it into reports that are submitted up the line. Because of missed deadlines and miscommunications over time, the receiving department starts demanding earlier and earlier submissions of the data, until the deadline is before the first department ever receives numbers from the field. It's easy for this kind of dispute to escalate, with the receiving department insisting it has to use the earlier deadline because it's been left holding the bag so many times in the past, and the other is always late anyway. Anyone not caught up in the conflict can see that it's dumb to ask for the numbers to be submitted before they exist. If you can maintain a calm affect and keep asking questions about what's driving the insistence (consistently late reports) and reframe to a shared interest (meaningful reports, filed on time), you are more likely to be able to solve the problem. Agreeing on the definition of the problem and finding common ground (timely reports) may also help your colleague back down from the sillier aspects of the demands to focus on problem solving. Her interest isn't having the numbers before you receive them—it's receiving them reliably, in time to do her part before she's left holding the bag for a late report.

Finding the common ground is the key to solving problems, so you have a starting place. Sometimes that space can be tenuous. Your job is to find and enlarge it so you can work constructively together.

Finding Common Ground in the Duplicate
Journal Submission Dilemma
In the matter of the simultaneous submission of a coauthored paper to two journals by a graduate student and his advisor, it's not hard to understand the perspective from which the advisor insisted they violate their signed promise to seek acceptance from one journal at a time. Gambling that they wouldn't get caught would seem to double the chance of much-needed, time-sensitive professional recognition for both authors. The risk felt remote because the likelihood of both publications accepting the manuscript was small. (In the small-world department, though, it wouldn't have been unlikely for both journals to use overlapping pools of reviewers, which neither the student nor the advisor considered.) Besides, the advisor told the student, they could always withdraw the paper from one of the journals if the other accepted it.

For the student, all this combined in a perfect storm of rationalization—"small risk of getting caught; no one is likely to find out; we really need this; it's not a very big violation anyway; journals aren't fair to authors; I'm not in charge; the boss says it's okay"—at the intersection of temptation, pressure, and ambition. The correct step would be to ask the second journal to suspend review once the first editor agreed to a reconsideration. How embarrassing it will be, though, if what that editor hears is your motivation ("Even while we submitted to you, we were hoping someone better would still take our paper") rather than your words ("After we submitted to you, we appealed to the other editor as a long shot. We were most surprised when he agreed to the appeal, so now we must ask you to suspend review while that appeal is pending"). Whatever the second editor hears, your self-report could increase the possibility that he or she will reject the paper without review, as there are always more papers than quality journals to print them. The research team would lose time in the review process while the clocks on the promotion package and graduation were ticking. Both felt pressure in the situation, and they wanted and needed that paper to succeed.

The student thought about how he would feel if he was on the other side of the situation, and if others found out. Instead of e-mailing the second journal to suspend review of the paper, which his advisor had objected to, he wrote the advisor an e-mail trying diplomatically to raise those issues:

> I've thought a lot about the situation in which we find ourselves with our article. As members of the scientific community, I think we need to apprise one of the editors of the situation, and here is why.
>
> If I were to find out that one of the big guys in the field had taken advantage of an unusual situation to double submit an article, I would feel like he was being slimy and deciding he didn't have to live by the same rules as the rest of us, and I wouldn't soon forget it. I would be angry and lose respect for him. Similarly, if I were to put time and energy into reviewing an article only to find that the authors were publishing it in another journal, I would be pretty pissed off.
>
> I know the current system of publishing is very hard for scientists, and it sometimes feels like a battle between us and the scientific publishing industry. However, there are a lot of other scientists involved in this process, and I think we owe it to them to behave as we would want them to.
>
> As corresponding author and head of the lab, this is your decision to make. As a friend and colleague, I'm asking you to consider notifying one of the editors that the situation has changed. I think it's the right thing to do.

The student was also prepared to seek advice from his dissertation committee members, quietly, if this appeal was not effective. It was a relief when the advisor acknowledged the points in the e-mail, and indicated that he was thinking about it. The student understood this as the advisor seeking a face-saving way to act. While the advisor was thinking, though, the second journal rejected the manuscript.

At one level, the advisor's approach to gaming the system worked; he got both journals to review the article at the same time and did not get caught.

Consider, though, what could have happened if the student had not gone on record with the advisor and the situation had progressed and was later discovered. Without the e-mail trail, it would not have been that hard for the advisor, who had already shown himself willing to play a little fast and loose with the rules and with truth, to blame the graduate student for the double submission. Blaming others, after all, is a time-honored response to getting caught with your hand in the cookie jar. The graduate student also has laid down a foundation that might possibly make the advisor less willing to take shortcuts with the student's work and reputation in the future.

Strategies for Approaching Dilemmas

Remember the 65 percent in the Milgram study who flipped the switches to administer shocks? Your choices can help you be more like one of the 35 percent who refused, rather than the majority who followed directions even when they were uncomfortable.

Safety Violation Obligations

You find a serious safety violation in an inspection. The employees who missed the problem are your friends and they really do not want your findings written up because it will affect them so badly. You think they mostly do a really good job and will be more careful from now on. Besides, if you report this, you'll lose the friendships. Write it up or look the other way?

What are the issues here? There are several, and the least obvious and perhaps most important one affects people who are not in the forefront of your considerations: those potentially affected by the safety violation. The people who are weighing on your mind are the friends who made the mistake, not the invisible (to you) people the inspections are meant to protect.

If you follow a structured decision-making approach by identifying the issues, rules, and regulations; articulating relevant questions; and reviewing options and those affected by each, the final step might alter your perspective. Considering those affected by possible safety violations, especially, the situation might look and feel differently to you. It's worth bearing in mind that sometimes choosing not to act is a decision, just as much as choosing to do something. If you see someone apparently hurt by the side of the road, for example, and are paralyzed, unable to decide what to do, you have just chosen not to help.

Here's what's most heartening about the Asch group pressure conformity studies, where the group confidently asserted the wrong answer and the subjects went along with them. Although at least 75 percent of subjects agreed with the obviously wrong answer at least once, if only one other person in the room gave the correct answer in opposition to the group, the overall conformity rate fell to just 5 percent.[8] Studies of altruism and the bystander effect show similar results. In staged circumstances with someone apparently in distress on the sidewalk, even one person stepping forward to help will elicit others to come forward and help as well.[9]

Individuals in stressful situations who are reminded (or remind themselves) that they are responsible for the consequences of their actions are more likely to resist bad orders from authority figures. Being mindful and prepared to decide can allow you to choose your path.

You can be that one person.

The tools and techniques we've covered, individually and in combination, can help you be a person who makes choices consistent with where you want to end up and shows the way for others as well. Do not outsource responsibility for your own choices.

Time Reporting Conundrum

Your boss instructs you to report no more than forty hours per week on your time sheet even though you both know you work more than that and there's a corporate policy mandating exact and accurate reporting of hours. What do you do with this pay period's time sheet?

Your options depend on the setting in which you are working: a multinational corporation in a regulated industry will have different practices than a mom-and-pop business. Your range of options as well as the most likely outcomes will turn on particulars.

In a large firm with a policy mandating accurate reporting of hours, not only does a pared-down report shortchange you, it skews the data used to estimate costs for future work, thus perpetuating the error and inflicting costs on others down the road. (Remember that broader thinking about the long-term effects of your choices will set you apart from others.) You know all of that, so your dilemma is how to take what you know to be the right course, not so much figuring out what that should be. Your first effort should always be to ask questions: maybe you misunderstood; maybe your boss miscommunicated; maybe there's something going on you don't understand. Have the policy close at hand when you raise the question—at a time convenient to the boss or maybe even via e-mail—in the mildest possible way about how to report the excess hours, because the project required more time than the policy permits. Your best resource in this case is likely to be an employee help line or problem-solving mechanism if your working environment has one and your relationship with the boss leaves you concerned about trying the direct route. Because employee work hours have serious external consequences for large businesses, even beyond the propagation of the problem into the future, prudence requires that you take some steps to go on record or get help.

If you're in a small family firm and your boss is the owner or a member of the family, other than asking questions or expressing concern, your choices are probably more limited: you can choose to do it or start looking for another job because there simply isn't much recourse that's sensible and proportionate. Not all problems have easy or good solutions. Rather than feeling manipulated, be sure that if you stay that it's a result of your own choice.

and making the parts in house, you could drop the supplier altogether. This would hurt the supplier, a longtime business partner. What do you do?

This is an interesting dilemma, one I've heard students argue both ways. If your loyalty is solely to your employees and shareholders, then you could say that saving money is worth losing a valued supplier. (Be sure your pencils are sharp enough to factor in all the costs of starting up the in-house process, and add the opportunity costs of the additional tasks and distractions.) If the relationship with your loyal supplier is important, or at least if breaching it in this way causes you concern, then other factors come into play.

A policy of transparency and good communication skills might help you work your way through the maze.

You could go to the supplier and say, "Here's the deal. Our business is under pressure to reduce costs. We think there's a legal way to get around using your patented technology that would save us money and we'd like to avoid harming our relationship. Perhaps we can talk." Part of seeing your way through this is to shift your perspective and see your supplier as an ally. Aligning your interests might serve both of you. Could your R&D folks work with the supplier to incorporate the cheaper manufacturing approach? Could you renegotiate the price? Is it worth something to you and your partner to be collaborating rather than contending over intellectual property?

Your path will depend on how you value the longtime relationship and your reputation as a business partner versus the bottom line. If you can improve one and maintain the other, wouldn't that be the best of both worlds?

End Up Where You Mean to Be

We stop at stop signs for a combination of reasons: to protect ourselves and others; to avoid the consequences of getting caught; because it's a habit; because of the Golden Rule; and as a component of community membership. Surviving and thriving in the professional world is the same. You do things to protect and advance yourself, for others, and to be a contributing member of the overlapping communities you simultaneously inhabit.

Where you end up will depend on how you start and upon all the choices, large and small, you make along the way. If you are aware of the many pitfalls in judgment to which we are all vulnerable and to learn to use available, effective tools, you can exert control over your destiny. Make the choices that will lead, by the end of your career, to feeling good about the work you've done, the reputation you've built, and the difference you've made in the lives of others, and with personal pride and satisfaction.

Here are the queries in your e-mail today. What are you going to do with each one?

1. When you were doing safety quality control, you noticed that all the reports you are being asked to sign and submit were obviously prepared all at one time, not daily as the regulations require. You queried your boss about it, and his response is awaiting you. His note says, "It's more efficient that way—just sign off and send it in." Now what?

2. One of your close friends from working at a previous employer together is also a client and has offered to take you on an all-expense-paid long weekend to Las Vegas. In her current position, she has purchasing responsibilities, among other things. Your friend has her "high-roller" status at the hotel, and the package includes travel and lodging for two. While you would not normally take such an offer from a client, she is also your friend. She is awaiting your response about going on the trip. What is your answer?

3. Your lead researcher in the marketing department asked to speak to you last week and revealed that she has come to believe that an hourly freelance interviewer faked all the

questionnaires he submitted. He's already been paid for the work. By company rules, all those interviews should be nullified and done over. If this is reported to the client and you order the interviews redone, your company will have to pay a penalty for breaking the contract, which will significantly damage the customer's confidence in your quality control process. Redoing the interviews will double the cost for a project that is already on a thin margin. You have a note from your lead researcher asking for your decision about what to do. How will you respond?

4. You have a message from the legal department:

We're tracking a potential leak about our acquisition strategy and need to rule people out before we start interviewing some of your subordinates. Could you please certify that you did not talk to anyone at Company A [a target for acquisition by your company] about our interest in it?

You stop to think carefully before responding, because you know that your response will be part of a legal file. You didn't talk to anyone at the company and can say so categorically. In thinking about it, though, you recall a conversation with one of your closest friends from college at lunch recently. She was confiding how much stress she and her husband were having over money. You told her that something good might be happening for him soon, and then said you couldn't say any more. Her husband works for the acquisition target and you were just trying to help an old friend. You didn't say anything specific, and you certainly didn't talk to anyone at the company. How do you reply?

5. Among other things, you oversee inventory management at a large warehouse in your division. Your boss has e-mailed you to let you know the external auditors are coming in next week. Your company has hired the auditors because it hopes to receive a large loan from a bank. You have raised concerns in the past about how your company tracks inventory, as you are worried

the systems in use do not provide consistent or accurate numbers. Your boss has specifically asked you to keep those concerns to yourself. You have a request from the auditors for a meeting. What will you say?

6. Your boss consistently gets your credentials wrong when he introduces you to people, saying you were in the top of your class and have a certification you do not have. You have corrected him (gently) many times, but he continues to make the mistake all the time. He seems proud that these qualifications (that you do not have) reflect well on him. He's on the program committee of a major industry meeting and has secured you a prestigious speaking spot at it. In your mail is the "save the date" advance publicity for the meeting. Your credentials are misrepresented in the tentative program. You're sure it's because your boss provided them as you have not yet been asked for any information by the organizers. What will you do?

This is not a test—this is your life.

Live it well.

APPENDIX

NOTES

SUGGESTED READING

ACKNOWLEDGMENTS

CREDITS

INDEX

APPENDIX

Reference Materials

Practicing the And Stance (inspired by William Ury)

Rephrase each of the following prompts to use "and," not "but" without changing the fundamental message.

1. The first five pages are very good, but your organization and argument deteriorate after that.
2. I'd like to be able to grant your request for a day off, but we will be short-staffed that day already.
3. That sounds like a fascinating story, but I just don't have time to listen.
4. This really shouldn't be turned into a legal situation, but we don't have a good solution yet.
5. I really thought it was going to be a terrible night, but it was actually quite nice.
6. This section is fine, but the rest needs to be reworked.
7. I'm very supportive of your candidacy, but I don't think I will be able to write a letter for you.
8. I did agree you could start looking at conferences, but not that many.

9. I have had terrible experiences with him in the past, but it sounds like a great opportunity for you.
10. I cannot agree with you, but you make a good point.
11. I appreciate your interest in the position, but you don't meet our minimum requirements.
12. Thank you for your interest in my work, but I'm unable to accept your invitation.

Personal Scripts Guidelines

Remember: The Rules for Having
Disputes at Work

- Consider Alternative Explanations (Especially That You May Be Wrong)
- In Light of Rule One, Ask Questions, Do Not Make Charges
- Figure Out What Documentation Supports Your Concerns and Where It Is
- Separate Your Personal and Professional Concerns
- Assess Your Goals
- Seek Advice and Listen to It

Guidelines

1. **Prepare.** Be ready to consider alternative explanations, especially that you might be wrong. Be as calm as possible. Assess your goals and match your actions to your goals.
2. **Open with a compliment and your request.** *"I admire the way you handle tough situations, and I am hoping that you might give me some advice on a situation I'm involved in now."*
3. **Leave time and conversational openings for the other to respond.** *"I'd like to explain my concerns and then I hope you will be willing to share your reactions with me."*
4. **Use neutral language to describe the situation.** *"I'd like to understand more about why . . ."* and soften your introductory phrases to leave room for a misunderstanding:

Yet Another Reimbursement Dilemma

> You're the lowest-status person at a business dinner that went way over allowable entertaining limits. Your manager asks you to pick up the check, instructing you to divide the expense into smaller segments and submit your vouchers to him for reimbursement over the next four or five months until it's all paid off.

This is one of those early forks in the road that will help define who you are to your manager and your coworkers. By now you should know that many companies routinely audit expenditures and discipline people who are found to be dishonest. Taking liberties in this area will put not only you but the manager at risk as well. (Companies take this stuff seriously. One semester, I hosted three high-level guest speakers who, unprompted, each told stories about having recently fired subordinates for fudging expense accounts. One was a CEO who discovered a request for reimbursement for a $400 dinner turned in by a vice president for entertaining at an industry trade show. It listed guests who had actually been at the CEO's own event that same evening.)

To carry out your manager's request, you'll need to falsify expense reports multiple times. This will demonstrate a clear pattern and intent if your actions are discovered. That's a serious offense likely to be quite harmful to your continued employment. Perhaps worse, your manager and everyone at the dinner will know that you are flexible about complying with rules, which isn't a great way to establish your reputation for honorable conduct with this group. It could easily open you to other, larger requests in the future.

When you're on the spot in the moment, if you have a delaying-to-buy-time-to-think script prepared, trot it out. In the best of all possible worlds, you'll have a values- or truth-based statement ready to use, too, like "This will put me over my credit limit," or "I have a big purchase coming up and just won't be able to carry this," or "I'd be so uncomfortable doing this, and I'm so bad at stuff like this, I'm sure I'll blow it."

There's not much downside in most jobs to be known to avoid untruths because you're a bad liar.

Leave Off Data Points?

Your advisor instructs you to leave off data points that "muddy up" the findings in a way you think is deceptive. Even after you point out that leaving them off changes the reality of the results, she persists. What do you do?

This is a classic "help me understand" moment in which you should be guarding against a sinister attribution bias. You do not know the advisor's motives and you might well have polluted the conversation the first time around if your question suggested you thought her request was rooted in a desire to deceive. You're the student. Your advisor is supposed to be teaching you, so asking dumb questions here is a perfect move. Circle back to the question at a low-stress moment and explain that you're confused and wish to understand. If you sense the advisor was offended by your wording the first time, apologize for expressing yourself clumsily. You still need much more information before you form conclusions.

If the answer leaves you still uncomfortable, it's time to seek advice from someone with more experience, perhaps a retired faculty member or a trusted member of your thesis committee. It is not only possible, it is likely that there are things you do not understand about the situation and exerting energy to uncover them is time well spent. All your questions should be framed as seeking to learn, as a way to remedy your misunderstanding. Being self-deprecating and owning ignorance are the way to go. The penalty for being uninformed is lower than that for bringing an unfounded accusation against someone who has a lot of control over your career. Follow the guidelines for handling disputes professionally, listening especially carefully to the responses you get.

If those you consult agree with your advisor, and their stated reasons don't compute for you, two possibilities to consider are that you do not understand the experiment or instrumentation well, or this is a not a good place for you to be. If it's the latter, and it's possible, you should explore switching labs. If those you consult agree with you, the best possible outcome is that one of them assists you in getting through the situation. Failing that, you may need to consult a grievance dean or ombudsperson or someone on your campus who might be able to advise you or provide assistance. You will need allies in this situation if you conclude you must pursue your concerns. If your name is to be on the publication and you cannot come to understand and agree with the step you're being directed to take, you may not have much choice but to involve others. If your name is not going to be on the publication, create a paper trail documenting your concerns, do the work, and start the process to find a place that is a better fit for your values and sensibilities.

Limits of Customer Service

> Imagine your team is on site with your best customer, installing software. While you're there, they ask you to fix a problem, which requires you to reboot the computer. You're more than happy to do it for them—until you realize that their copy of their operating system is not legal.

Your action to install (or not) software on top of an illegal system will highlight clearly what you and your company stand for. Demonstrating willingness to cheat another company by violating its license terms would send a very strong message. It would reveal hypocrisy in your company and invite unhealthy reciprocity from your customer. If the customer is big enough to justify your buying a legal copy of the operating system, do just that and tell the customer what you did. If your budget doesn't permit such a purchase, check with your boss, as an element of good boss management and to have the weight of your company behind your choice. Do a quick read-up on the legal consequences for corporations of knowingly pirating software if you anticipate that your boss might flinch, and, if necessary, do it all in writing so you have a paper trail (and to reduce the chance your boss will try to look the other way).

One way out is to offer nicely to install a legal version if your customer pays for it. If the customer won't do so, and the boss backs you, then decline the request to fix the computer with a gentle tone with a factual, low emotional temperature. Explain the principled basis for your refusal calmly, and nothing about the situation should rebound negatively on you or your company.

Sales Competition

> Your little sister, working in retail, has an urgent request for advice. "Our chain is having a sales competition, and my general manager has asked everyone in our store to buy expensive merchandise on our personal credit cards and then to return it to other stores in the chain in our region to help our numbers look better at the end of the quarter. We'll all get a bonus for being the highest-volume store. What do I do?"

Labeling this for what it is (and explaining what shell games like this mean for the larger corporation) may help. An even faster response might be to ask questions. What's your little sister's credit limit? Does she even have to take this issue on directly? Can she just say that she doesn't have any room on her credit card to make an expensive purchase? Unless she plans to make a career of working in this chain (note to yourself for another day: think about your advice to her on finding a different ladder to climb, as this one sounds pretty shaky), her best bet may be to avoid being involved in the first place, however appealing the bonus might be.

If your sister's credit is good enough to make the initial purchase, she could well be faced with making a decision and developing a personal script to implement whatever advice you provide, which will help to define you to your sister and vice versa.

Limits to Reverse Engineering?

> Your R&D department presents a proposal that could replace a supplier's patented technology and avoid royalties, with a 10 percent reduction in manufacturing costs. By changing the materials used

6. This section is fine, but the rest needs to be reworked.

   This section is fine and with a bit more more revision, the rest can be just as good.

7. I'm very supportive of your candidacy, but I don't think I will be able to write a letter for you.

   I'm very supportive of your candidacy and you would do better to ask someone who knows your work better in the area of their particular interest.

   I'm very supportive of your candidacy, and I'm not the right person to write for you as I do not have a strong relationship with (the addressee).

   I'm very supportive of your candidacy and want to make sure that you know my letter will need to include your showing in my class.

8. I did agree you could start looking at conferences, but not that many.

   I did agree you could start looking at conferences, and now let's refine your list to the two most important.

   I did agree you could start looking at conferences and I'd like to see you focus in on one or two that will do the most for improving your work-related skills.

   I did agree you could start looking at conferences and our policy is that our office pays for one conference a year for professional development. Which one looks best to you?

9. I have had terrible experiences with him in the past, but it sounds like a great opportunity for you.

   I have had terrible experiences with him in the past and that might have been about our chemistry and wouldn't affect how things would go for you.

10. I cannot agree with you, but you make a good point.

I cannot agree with you and your good point is one that I'll keep thinking about.

I cannot agree with you and hope that we can keep talking, as your point is a good one.

11. I appreciate your interest in the position, but you don't meet our minimum requirements.

I appreciate your interest in the position and I hope you'll apply again when you there's a better match between the advertised minimum requirements and your experience.

I appreciate your interest in the position and wish that we were not restricted to the minimum requirements advertised. I hope you'll keep watching and apply again.

I appreciate your interest in the position and hope the application process has been educational for you, especially about the importance of watching the minimum requirements stated.

12. Thank you for your interest in my work, but I'm unable to accept your invitation.

Thank you for your interest in my work and I'm sorry I'm unable to accept your invitation.

Thank you for your interest in my work and I'm sorry the scheduling just won't work this year. I hope you'll ask again.

Thank you for your interest in my work and I hope your conference goes very well. I'm unable to accept your invitation this time around.

Notes

Prologue

1. Wendy Fischman, Becca Solomon, Deborah Schutte, and Howard Gardner, *Making Good: How Young People Cope with Moral Dilemmas at Work* (Cambridge, MA: Harvard University Press, 2004), 23.

1. Start As You Mean to Go On

1. P. Gardner, "Moving Up or Moving Out of the Company. Factors That Influence the Promoting or Firing of New College Hires," Michigan State University Collegiate Employment Research Institute Research Brief 1-2007.
2. R. M. Kidder, "Trust: A Primer on Current Thinking," Institute for Global Ethics Research Report. Available at http://www.globalethics.org /files/wp_trust_1222960968.pdf/21/.
3. J. M. Darley and C. D. Batson, " 'From Jerusalem to Jericho': A Study of Situational and Dispositional Variables in Helping Behavior," *Journal of Personality and Social Psychology* 27 (1973): 100–108.
4. Eugene M. Caruso and Francesca Gino, "Blind Ethics: Closing One's Eyes Polarizes Moral Judgments and Discourages Dishonest Behavior," *Cognition* 118, no. 2 (February 2011): 280–285.
5. Robert B. Cialdini, Petria K. Petrova, and Noah J. Goldstein, "The Hidden Costs of Organizational Dishonesty," *MIT Sloan Management Review* (Spring 2004): 42–49.
6. Ibid.
7. J. Jennings and K. Casey, *In God's Care: Daily Meditations on Spirituality in Recovery* (Center City, MN: Hazelden Foundation, 1991).
8. Federal Trade Commission, "FTC Publishes Final Guides Governing Endorsements, Testimonials: Changes Affect Testimonial Advertisements, Bloggers, Celebrity Endorsements," October 5, 2009. Available at http://www.ftc.gov/opa/2009/10/endortest.shtm. Code of Federal Regulations 16 CFR Part 255, p. 53124, Vol. 74, No. 98, October 15, 2009.

9. W. James, *Principles of Psychology*, Vol. 2 (Mineola, NY: Dover Publications, 1950).

10. John D. Bransford, Ann L. Brown, and Rodney R. Cocking, eds., *How People Learn: Brain, Mind, Experience, and School* (Washington, DC: National Academies Press, 1999). Available at http://www.nap.edu /openbook.php?isbn=0309070368.

11. G. Easton and T. C. Ormerod, Final Report to the Case Clearing House (February, 2001). Available at http://www.ecch.com/files/downloads /research/RP0303M.pdf.

12. Karen S. Hill, "Improving Quality and Patient Safety by Retaining Nursing Expertise," *OIJN: The Online Journal of Issues in Nursing* 15, no. 3 (August 2, 2010). Available at http://www.nursingworld.org /MainMenuCategories/ANAMarketplace/ANAPeriodicals/OJIN /TableofContents/Vol152010/No3-Sept-2010/Articles-Previously-Topic /Improving-Quality-and-Patient-Safety-.html.

13. Donald L. Wass and William Oncken Jr., "Management Time: Who's Got the Monkey?," *Harvard Business Review* (November–December 1974).

2. Develop a Professional Persona

1. "The free expression by outward signs of an emotion intensifies it. On the other hand, the repression, as far as this is possible, of all outward signs softens our emotions. Even the simulation of an emotion tends to arouse it in our minds." Charles Darwin, *The Expression of Emotions in Men and Animals* (London: John Murray, 1872).

2. Eugene M. Caruso and Francesca Gino, "Blind Ethics: Closing One's Eyes Polarizes Moral Judgments and Discourages Dishonest Behavior," *Cognition* 118 (2011): 280–285.

3. Amy Drahota, Alan Costall, and Vasudevi Reddy, "The Vocal Communication of Different Kinds of Smile," *Speech Communication* 50, no. 4 (2008): 278–287.

4. Rob Cross, Wayne Baker, and Andrew Parker, "What Creates Energy in Organizations?," *MIT Sloan Management Review* (Summer 2000): 51–56.

5. Brad Tuttle, "Warren Buffett's Boring, Brilliant Wisdom," *Time* (March 1, 2010). Available at http://moneyland.time.com/2010/03/01/warren -buffetts-boring-brilliant-wisdom/.

6. Peter F. Drucker, "Managing Oneself," *Harvard Business Review* 77, no. 2 (1999): 64–74.

7. W. W. Burke and G. H. Litwin, "A Causal Model of Organizational Performance and Change," *Journal of Management* 18, no. 3 (1992): 523–545.

8. Robert Sutton, *The No Asshole Rule: Building a Civilized Workplace and Surviving One That Isn't* (New York: Business Plus, 2007).

9. Ibid., 152.

10. Arijit Chatterjee and Donald Hambrick, "It's All about Me: Narcissistic Chief Executive Officers and Their Effects on Company Strategy and Performance," *Administrative Science Quarterly* 52 (2007): 351–386.

11. Michael Maccoby, "Narcissistic Leaders: The Incredible Pros, the Inevitable Cons," *Harvard Business Review* (January 2004): 1–10. For additional information, see Michael Maccoby, *Narcissistic Leaders: Who Succeeds and Who Fails* (Allston, MA: Harvard Business Review Press, 2007).

12. Mary Kay Haben, Leighton Lecture on Leadership and Ethics, University of Illinois. March 26, 2008. Transcript and PowerPoint available at http://www.business.illinois.edu/responsibility/news/2008/03-26-leighton-lecture.html.

3. Why Things Go Wrong

1. Stanley Milgram, "Behavioral Study of Obedience," *Journal of Abnormal and Social Psychology* 67, no. 4 (1963): 371–378. For further information, see this video of the original experiment, http://www.you tube.com/watch?v=8olVHKgIBXc&feature=related.

2. Francesca Gino and Max S. Bazerman, "When Misconduct Goes Unnoticed: The Acceptability of Graduate Erosion in Others' Unethical Behavior," *Journal of Experimental Social Psychology* 45, no. 4 (2009): 708–719.

3. Dan Ariely, *The Honest Truth About Dishonesty: How We Lie to Everyone—Especially Ourselves* (New York: HarperCollins, 2012), 58.

4. Ibid., 34.

5. James M. Tyler, Robert S. Feldman, and Andreas Reichert, "The Price of Deceptive Behavior: Disliking and Lying to People Who Lie to Us," *Journal of Experimental Social Psychology* 42, no. 1 (2004): 69–77; Nathanael J. Fast and Larissa Z. Tiedens, "Blame Contagion: The Automatic Transmission of Self-Serving Attributions," *Journal of Experimental Social Psychology* 46, no. 1 (2010): 97–106.

6. P. G. Zimbardo, "The Power and Pathology of Imprisonment," *Congressional Record*, Serial No. 15, 1971-10-25 (Washington, DC: U.S. Government Printing Office). For further information, see http://www.youtube.com/watch?v=oC5hl1BLUiw&feature=related.

7. James W. Pennebaker, *The Secret Life of Pronouns: What Our Words Say about Us* (London: Bloomsbury Press, 2011), 232.

8. Solomon Asch, "Studies in the Principles of Judgments and Attitudes: II. Determination of Judgments by Group and Ego Standards," *Journal of Social Psychology* 12 (1940): 433–465. For further information, see http://www.youtube.com/watch?v=iRh5qy09nNw.

9. Stanley Milgram, "Behavioral Study of Obedience," *Journal of Abnormal and Social Psychology* 67, no. 4 (1963): 371–378.

10. Robert B. Cialdini, Petria K. Petrova, and Noah J. Goldstein, "The Hidden Costs of Organizational Dishonesty," *MIT Sloan Management Review* (Spring 2004): 42–49.

11. Steven Kerr, "On the Folly of Rewarding A, While Hoping for B," *Academy of Management Executive* 9, no. 1 (February 1995): 7–14.

12. Peter F. Drucker, "Managing Oneself," *Harvard Business Review* (January 1, 2005): 102–114.

13. Marilee Jones and Kenneth R. Ginsburg, *Less Stress, More Success: A New Approach to Guiding Your Teen through College Admissions and Beyond* (Elk Grove, IL: American Academy Of Pediatrics, 2006), 197.

14. Marcella Bombardieri, "Ex-MIT Dean Never Cited Actual Degree," *Boston Globe,* May 2, 2007. Available at http://www.boston.com/news/education/higher/articles/2007/05/02/ex_mit_dean_never_cited_actual_degree/.

15. G. B. Hickson, E. W. Clayton, P. B. Githens, and F. A. Sloan, "Factors That Prompted Families to File Medical Malpractice Claims Following Perinatal Injuries," JAMA 267, no. 10 (1992): 1359–1363.

16. Leslie Wayne, "Raytheon Chief's Management Rules Have a Familiar Ring," *New York Times,* April 24, 2006.

17. Not every story has a sad ending. Raytheon withdrew the book and penalized Swanson by cutting his compensation by $1 million. He is still the CEO. Evidently the Raytheon board ultimately concluded, when they fined him but kept him on as CEO, that they could live with a plagiarist as their leader. The calculus must have involved deciding that taking credit for work not his own was not central to Swanson's ability to perform effectively as CEO. (Or maybe it is?) Del Jones, "Executive Suite: Raytheon CEO Turns Lessons Learned into Hit Booklet," *USA Today,* December 18, 2005. Available at http://www.usatoday.com/money/companies/management/2005-12-18-raytheon-advice_x.htm.

18. College Board, Student Descriptive Questionnaire (Princeton, NJ: Educational Testing Service, 1976–1977), in Dunning and Gilovich, *How We Know What Isn't So* (New York: The Free Press, 1991).

19. K. Patricia Cross, "Not Can, but Will College Teaching Be Improved?" *New Directions for Higher Education,* no. 17 (1977): 1–15.

20. Justin Kruger and David Dunning, "Unskilled and Unaware of It: How Difficulties in Recognizing One's Own Incompetence Lead to Inflated

Self-Assessments," *Journal of Personality and Social Psychology* 77, no. 6 (1999): 1121–1134.

21. Barry Bearak, "The Living Nightmare. Quanitta Underwood: A Contender for Olympic Gold and a Survivor," *New York Times*, February 11, 2012, 7–31.

4. How Things Go Right

1. Oxford Corpus, "The OEC: Facts about the language," Oxford Dictionaries, http://oxforddictionaries.com/words/the-oec-facts-about-the-language (accessed February 25, 2012).

5. How to Have a Dispute Professionally

1. Sukhwinder S. Shergill, Paul M. Bays, Chris D. Frith, and Daniel M. Wolpert, "Two Eyes for an Eye: The Neuroscience of Force Escalation," *Science* 301, no. 5630 (2003): 187.
2. John M. Darley and Bibb Latané, "Bystander Intervention in Emergencies: Diffusion of Responsibility," *Journal of Personality and Social Psychology* 8, no. 4 (1968): 377–383.

6. Stay on the High Road

1. Michael M. Harris and John Schaubroeck, "A Meta-Analysis of Self-Supervisor, Self-Peer, and Peer-Supervisor Ratings," *Personnel Psychology* 41, no. 1 (1988): 43–63, as cited in David Dunning, *Self-Insight: Roadblocks and Detours on the Path to Knowing Thyself* (New York: Psychology Press, 2005), 5.
2. Bernard M. Bass and Francis J. Yammerino, "Congruence of Self and Others' Leadership Ratings of Naval Officers for Understanding Successful Performance," *Applied Psychology* 40, no. 4 (1991): 154–157, as cited in Dunning, *Self-Insight*, 5.
3. Peter Medawar, "The Strange Case of the Spotted Mice," *New York Review of Books* 23 (1976): 6–11.
4. Peter F. Drucker, "Managing Oneself," *Harvard Business Review* 77, no. 2 (1999): 64–74.
5. C. E. Naquin, T. R. Kurtzberg, and L. Y. Belkin, "The Finer Points of Lying: E-mail vs. Pen and Paper," *Journal of Applied Psychology* 95, no. 2 (2010): 387–394.
6. The Innocence Project, "Innocence Blog: Illinois Man Released after Attorneys Reveal Another Man's Confession," (April 21, 2008). Available at http://www.innocenceproject.org/Content/Illinois_man_released _after_attorneys_reveal_another_mans_confession.php.

7. Unlike the other scenarios in this book, this is not a situation about which I have personal knowledge; it was still on the whiteboard in a classroom where I gave a visiting lecture many years ago at UT Galveston; despite repeated efforts, I was never able to find the instructor who had posed it, and I assume it was, like so many dilemmas posed to medical students, a real person's dilemma. A tip of the hat to its originator.

8. Solomon Asch, "Studies in the Principles of Judgments and Attitudes: II. Determination of Judgments by Group and Ego Standards," *Journal of Social Psychology* 12 (1940): 433–465.

9. John M. Darley and Bibb Latané, "Bystander Intervention in Emergencies: Diffusion of Responsibility," *Journal of Personality and Social Psychology* 8, no. 4 (1968): 377–383; Bibb Latané and Steve Nida, "Ten Years of Research on Group Size and Helping," *Psychological Bulletin* 89, no. 2 (1981): 308–324.

Suggested Reading

Foundational Materials for Career Success

Joseph L. Badaracco, "Discipline of Building Character," *Harvard Business Review,* March 2009.

    A concise article providing ways to think about your core values and career choices.

Rob Cross, Wayne Baker, and Andrew Parker, "What Creates Energy in Organizations?," *MIT Sloan Management Review,* July 2003.

    Knowing about energizers and de-energizers and how they affect those with whom they interact is a key idea to understand and internalize for long-term success in working with other people.

P. Drucker, "Managing Oneself," *Harvard Business Review,* January 2008.

    A classic in the business literature, Drucker's advice applies across fields, and every professional would benefit from considering his advice about taking charge of your career and thinking about how you can play to your strengths.

Carol S. Dweck, "Caution—Praise Can Be Dangerous," *American Educator,* Spring 1999.

    How you praise people affects their motivation. Read and consider.

W. Oncken and D. Wass, "Management Time: Who's Got the Monkey?," *Harvard Business Review,* November 1999.

    Another classic article, it introduces the concept of different kinds of demands on your time and ways to think about managing them—and yourself.

Robert I. Sutton, "The No Asshole Rule," *Business Plus,* 2007.

    Life is too short to work with horrible people who are de-energizers, or worse. This has good advice for assessing yourself and tools for dealing with awful colleagues and bosses; provides food for thought when you're in charge and what kind of people you recruit, retain, and reward.

Specific Skills and Ideas

W. Ury, *Getting Past No: Negotiating Your Way from Confrontation to Cooperation* (New York: Bantam, 1993).

> This is my favorite negotiation book. It's practical, accessible, and wise. It's worth reading once a year or so.

Kendall Zoller and Claudette Landry, *The Choreography of Presenting* (Thousand Oaks, CA: Sage, 2010).

> If you make presentations or speak in front of people, the knowledge and experience presented here are valuable.

Understanding Ourselves and Others

Dan Ariely, *The Honest Truth About Dishonesty: How We Lie to Everyone—Especially Ourselves* (New York: Harper, 2012).

> We all like to think we're honest, and yet we cut corners here and there. A thought-provoking book that includes ways to be as honest as we think of ourselves being.

Max H. Bazerman and Ann E. Tenbrunsel, *Blind Spots* (Princeton, NJ: Princeton University Press, 2011).

> Ethical decision making is harder than it seems. Detailed information based on research about biases and decision making in the ethical arena. Arm yourself with solid information and ways to buttress choices that match your values.

Robert Cialdini, *Influence: Science and Practice,* 4th Ed. (Boston: Allyn and Bacon, 2001).

> Summarizes key research and findings in social psychology in an accessible way for understanding influence and persuasion.

Charles Duhigg, *The Power of Habit* (New York: Random House, 2012).

> If you want your decisions to match your values, the habits you cultivate will play a major role in your success—or not.

James W. Pennebaker, *The Secret Life of Pronouns* (London: Bloomsbury, 2011).

> Our language reveals more about us—and others—than we might think.

Douglas Stone, Bruce Patton, and Sheila Heen, *Difficult Conversations* (New York: Penguin, 2010).

> While the book focuses on difficult conversations in personal life, the skills are also useful at work.

Carol Tavris and Elliot Aronson, *Mistakes Were Made (But Not by Me)* (Boston: Houghton Mifflin Harcourt, 2007).

> How we deceive ourselves and how to overcome the biases we all have in decision making.

Acknowledgments

If writing a book is a journey, this one was like a group tour that took the scenic route. It did so for reasons that were inside my head, literally: somewhere in the middle of this project, I had surgery to remove a large brain tumor. Thankfully, it was benign, and that particular side trip was not without interest, unplanned as it was. I had devoted companions along on the tour, and to them, I owe much. My family was with me every step of the way, as was a community of loving friends and caring students and colleagues. The stalwart friends who supported me through this period of my life were, well, lifesavers. They encouraged and cared for me throughout. The details are a story for another time and place and include everything from covering my classes and speaking obligations that couldn't be moved, to walking our dogs so their exuberance didn't trip me at home, to bringing chocolate sauce and other healing potions and cheering me through the recovery process.

Along this journey, this caring group read many (many) incarnations of this book as I struggled to recover not just physically, but also my written voice and direction. I owe much to Elizabeth Knoll, editor extraordinaire. Her wisdom, skill, and perspicacity are widely known and appreciated. She's also funny, patient, and kind, not to mention a fellow Midwesterner at heart; if you've been inculcated in that mindset, you know what I mean. I am deeply indebted to Elizabeth for hanging with me through a strange and unpredictable interlude, especially across the several false starts when I was refiguring out how to produce coherent, readable text. All resulting shortcomings are mine, remaining in spite of her coaching and the contributions of all those to whom I owe so much.

Friends and students read multiple false starts at what eventually became this book, and they steered me back to a better course when they saw me detouring. Mary Ellen O'Shaughnessey and Nancy McCowen, in particular, helped discern the real book hiding in a messy early draft and were guides to what they saw as the needs of young professionals from their double-vantage of supervisors and mothers. Deb Aronson helped me find a way to shape that book through many resulting drafts. Doug Brown and David Frankel read versions of later drafts, thought about the ethical and practical problems they contained, and raised other problems from their experiences in Silicon Valley and beyond. As always, Doug used humor to highlight evasive insights, and David brought his incisive views to bear in ways that improved the final product. From our discussions emerged a wonderful collaboration in which David came to interact with classes and budding entrepreneurs at the College of Business at the University of Illinois, which has been enriching for me as a teacher and for many a student.

My teaching partner in Business 101, Gretchen Winter, brought experience and perspectives that strengthened connections to the world and people of business, and was patient and generous while my attention was sometimes distracted by book stuff. She reality-tested the book's advice and helped develop good or better answers to dilemmas in it. Cindy Workman Hyden worked with me through a total restructuring of the emerging book, which resulted in taking an entire draft apart and reassembling it in closer to the final form. Fred Delcomyn read a complete draft with his usual care, making connections and catching problems I'd become blind to during the long journey. His comments were characteristically thought-provoking and helpful in improving the final product. Sanaz Mobaseri provided some real-world perspective; Starza Kolman and Gene Amberg provided comments. Jovanna Stanley served as cheerleader, sounding board, and grammar maven throughout the life of this project. She helped untangle impossible sentences and got me to think through what I really meant, as well as brought her irrepressible life passion and verve to the process. Jovanna always was available to help or listen, even at very busy times in her life. Personally and professionally, she made this project better.

This book would not exist without Billy Tabrizi. He read every word of every draft, made hugely valuable and constructive suggestions (over and over), helped track down references, suggested topics, and persuaded me there was a need for the book and that I should keep going when my confidence flagged. I've been learning from and enjoying knowing Billy since he took a negotiation class with me in his first semester in college. My interactions with him have enriched my teaching and my writing—and my faith in the future. The world is in good hands with Billy and his peers.

Billy's peers include all the other wonderful students, especially at the College of Business at Illinois in recent years, who have taught me and contributed in so many ways to my work: Evan Thompson and Jenna Myers were generous with their time and energy, reading and commenting on a draft at a pivotal moment with a resulting needed sharpening of focus. Stephanie Soles had insights and energy that shaped my thinking and helped me cover all my bases. The cohorts of Bus 101 Section Leaders who were committed to learning about and conveying concepts of professional responsibility showed me what mattered the most to students, as did the MBA students in the program at Illinois in my Ethics and Leadership class.

If it weren't for Larry DeBrock, Dean of the College, and Greg Northcraft and Victor Mullins, I would never have met all these great students; I owe them all, and especially Larry for his commitment to the foundational value of ethics and professional responsibility in the curriculum. Nick Petruzzi extends and builds on that commitment in the MBA program, and Courtney Grussing helps make it all work. My good fortune and the privilege of contributing to business education had its roots in working with John Hedeman in the 1990s. Watching John as he built the undergraduate honors program at Illinois has been a pleasure, and I'm grateful for his friendship throughout, as well as his thoughtful comments on the manuscript as it finally emerged.

Business 101 wouldn't have come together without the contributions of a large number of people, from the original faculty committee who conceived of the program through the Office of Undergraduate Affairs staff who make it happen, and members of the course management team over the years: Madhu Viswanathan, Pnina Steiner and her great BCS colleagues, Ruth Badger, Deanna Dale, Celeste Richardson, Colette Niland, Pat Shell, Billy Tabrizi, Nick Timpone, Joy Daniel, Starza Kolman, Devin Ruthstrom, Abby Sullivan, Stephanie Barry, Brad Pnazek, and Chris Angelica.

I'm especially indebted to those who contributed experiences or dilemmas presented in one way or another in the book and for their permission to use them here with the aim of helping others. Those include Winmay Au, Brad Baas, Steve Beckett, Fahad Zia Chaudhary, Won Choi, David Frankel, David George, Christopher Greene, Kearney Gunsalus, Erin Ha, Lisa Huson, David Ikenberry, Siddharth Juneja, Min Gu Jung, Craig Kitching, Kim Kloepper, Katrina (Shih-Yang) Lin, Joan Lin, Alan Marsh, Jordy McNamara, Sumeet Mittal, Sanaz Mobasseri, Christopher Mulliken, Ron Myers, Mary Ellen O'Shaughnessey, Brian Parrino, Michael Petrik, Kyle Pietila, Swetha Ravi, Sultan Salim, Paul Stancil, Dylan Stark, Susan Starrett, Harriett Weatherford, Robert Wengert, and Gretchen Winter. There are several more who asked not to be named, and that they are not listed does not diminish the value of their contribution or my gratitude. This group includes the unnamed instructor at the University of Texas Galveston who left the kidney transplant dilemma on the whiteboard in a room in which I later lectured. That scenario is the only one in the book that did not come to me in person, and I tried many a time to track down its source, without any success. Whoever you are, your teaching catalyzed scores of great conversations across my dinner table and in classrooms over two decades: thank you.

Ron Myers has become a good friend and colleague. We met through one of the Illinois MBAs, Kristin Lisa, to whom I'm indebted for making the connection. Ron's business perspective and his commitment to professional responsibility and ethical leadership, and his willingness and enthusiasm in sharing them with students has positively affected many students and informed my own thinking.

Finally, and always, my teachers at home, Kearney and Anna Shea, have shaped me for the better as a mother, as a teacher, and as a person. Their lessons permeate this book and my life in ways I celebrate every day. Kearney read and commented on the most problematic versions and helped me find my way through the thickets. Her engagement with the issues at the core of the book has sharpened my thinking over many years, and her astute view of the nuances and subtleties always enriches my thinking. Shea's feedback was inimitably her own, unvarnished, straightforward, constructive, and loving.

This book, as with all else over the last thirty-five years, begins and ends with my partnership with Michael. It makes my work possible and better, and my life joyful.

Credits

Portions of Chapter 5 first appeared in my article "How to Blow the Whistle and Still Have a Career Afterwards," published in *Science and Engineering Ethics* 4 (1998). I am grateful for permission to use the material here.

Index